SOCIAL STUDIES,
LITERACY,
and
SOCIAL JUSTICE
in the
COMMON CORE
CLASSROOM

A Guide for Teachers

SOCIAL STUDIES, LITERACY, and SOCIAL JUSTICE in the COMMON CORE CLASSROOM
A Guide for Teachers

Ruchi Agarwal-Rangnath

Foreword by Christine Sleeter

Teachers College, Columbia University
New York and London

Published by Teachers College Press, 1234 Amsterdam Avenue, New York, NY 10027

Grateful acknowledgment is made for permission to reprint the following:

In Chapter 2, "America has power, but not justice." From Him Mark Lai, Genny Lim, and Judy Yung, *Island Poetry and History of Chinese Immigrants on Angel Island, 1910–1940.* Seattle: University of Seattle Press, 1991.

In Chapter 3, Figure 3.1, "Friendly Indians" by Antonio Herra. From Cecil Jane, *Select Documents Illustrating the Four Voyages of Columbus, Vol. 1.* London: The Hakluyt Society, 1929.

Library of Congress Cataloging-in-Publication Data

Agarwal-Rangnath, Ruchi.
    Social studies, literacy, and social justice in the common core classroom : a teachers' guide
    Ruchi Agarwal-Rangnath ; foreword by Christine Sleeter.
        pages cm
    Includes bibliographical references and index.
    ISBN 978-0-8077-5408-5 (pbk.)
    1. Social sciences—Study and teaching (Elementary) 2. Language arts—Correlation with content subjects. 3. Social justice—Study and teaching (Elementary) I. Title.
    LB1584.A366 2013
    372.83044—dc23

                                                                    2012047516

ISBN 978-0-8077-5408-5 (paper)

Printed on acid-free paper

Manufactured in the United States of America

20 19 18 17 16 15 14 13   8 7 6 5 4 3 2 1

Contents

Foreword

WE LIVE IN a time when social studies has virtually disappeared from so many classrooms—a time, ironically, when it is needed more than ever due to the rapid changes in society and a growing divisiveness that thwarts addressing those changes constructively. In this book, Ruchi Agarwal-Rangnath offers a much-needed vision for how social studies can be connected with language arts in the standards-based classroom, and how it can be designed and taught in a way that prepares young people to become actively engaged citizens with a social justice consciousness.

We need social studies that is grounded in social justice to prepare young people to live within, navigate, and embrace the growing diversity of the U.S. population. In May of 2012, Americans learned that more than half of all babies born in the United States now are of color. For the first time since the sixteenth century, White births are in a minority. While the growing diversity of the U.S. population comes as no surprise, the birthrate report prompted a variety of sentiments.

Some Americans, such as Patrick Buchanan (2012), lamented, "White America is a dying tribe." Others greeted the news pragmatically, such as an editorial writer in the *Fort Wayne News Sentinel* (2012), who wrote: "We will become a little less of what we were and a little more American all the time, changing what 'American' means in the process." The demographic shift has implications for how Americans view each other. As reported in *Aljazeera* (Halkett, 2012), the nation will probably experience increased tensions for another generation or so between Whites and non-Whites, especially among people who are uncomfortable with change. Helping young people view diversity as normal would represent a step forward. The demographic shift will also have policy implications. Commenting on "implications for the nation's economy, politics and identity," Trounson (2012) wrote that "a widening gap in ages between Whites and minorities, for example, could affect policies and funding for Social Security, child care and health services."

While young people can learn in any subject area to think creatively and constructively about issues inherent in a highly multicultural democracy, social studies is uniquely designed to focus on social issues and relationships. In addition, social studies is essential for preparing young people to work for equity and justice, especially given the current huge disparities across communities. Most Americans are aware of the well-documented rapidly growing gap between rich and poor. While few deny that an economic gap is growing, there is little consensus over whether it is a problem or not, and if so, what to do about it. Significantly, however, Tavis Smiley warns that, if Americans do not address "the economy for the 99 percent," not only will millions of Americans suffer, but the United States itself is in danger of losing its place as a world leader (Landes, 2012, p. 2). Figuring out how to bring about a more just distribution of economic resources will be an important task of next generations.

This book is designed to empower both teachers and students. It empowers teachers by offering a conceptual framework for curriculum planning in the context of state and Common Core language arts standards and by presenting numerous practical teaching strategies that teachers can use as tools in their classrooms. The book also empowers teachers by showing how literacy instruction can contribute to and build on social studies instruction. In other words, these two subject areas can be made to work together, even while fulfilling mandated minutes of literacy instruction. Vivid vignettes of classroom teachers show how practicing teachers have grappled with issues of social justice, curriculum standards, marginalization of social studies, and complexities of teaching in classrooms in diverse settings. For teachers whose students come from backgrounds unlike their own, the insights and strategies this book offers are especially valuable, making the vision of engaged teaching and learning in a culturally and intellectually complex classroom within reach.

Social Studies, Literacy, and Social Justice in the Common Core Classroom also empowers students. Students become empowered as their teachers learn to engage their sense of wonder, teach them to gather and piece together information to create and share their own interpretations of history, then guide them in acting on what they have learned. As teachers learn to open up students' questions and build on what students know, classroom instruction becomes more meaningful. When reading and writing are meaningful, students are able to use these as tools for their own learning. As students learn to unpack and delve into social issues that have meaning to their lives and then to act on issues in a way that is consistent with participatory democracy, they become empowered.

Throughout this book, Ruchi Agarwal-Rangnath grounds her analysis, framework, and suggested strategies in her own experience as a teacher, current research and theory in social studies and language arts methods, and the voices of classroom teachers. If you are a teacher, or are preparing to become a teacher, this is a book you will want to keep so that you can refer back to it again and again. If you are a teacher educator, this is a book that will help you connect demands on teachers today with a compelling vision of academically rich, student-centered social justice teaching. In either case, you are in for a treat.

—*Christine Sleeter,*
California State University Monterey Bay

REFERENCES

Buchanan, P. J. (2012, May 18). Has the bell begun to toll for the GOP? *Patrick J. Buchanan Official Website*. Retrieved from http://buchanan.org/blog/has-the-bell-begun-to-toll-for-the-gop-5077

Editorial: "Majority" may be changing, but we are still American. [Editorial]. (2012, May 21). *Fort Wayne (IN) News-Sentinel.com*. Retrieved from http://www.news-sentinel.com/apps/pbcs.dll/article?AID=/20120521/EDITORIAL/120529963

Halkett, K. (2012, May 18). America's new minority majority. *Aljazeera*. Retrieved from http://blogs.aljazeera.com/americas/2012/05/18/americas-new-minority-majority

Landes, L. (2012, May 18). Poverty is a threat to democracy. *Forbes*. Retrieved from http://www.forbes.com/sites/moneybuilder/2012/05/18/poverty-is-a-threat-to-democracy

Trounson, R. (2012, May 18). U.S. reaches historic demographic tipping point. *Los Angeles Times*. Retrieved from http://www.latimes.com/news/local/la-me-census-births-20120518,0,5678651.story

Preface

MANY BEGINNING TEACHERS and experienced teachers alike share the struggle of navigating standards and test-driven environments to develop social justice curriculum. Social justice curriculum is complex and difficult; it requires us to lean on our own creativity and understandings to make informed choices about what is best for the students. Moreover, teaching for social justice often requires us to bring in outside resources to deepen students' knowledge about social studies content areas. In this respect, teaching for social justice is definitely not a clear cut road. It requires creativity, ingenuity, understanding, passion, and fortitude.

As a teacher educator, I found most of my students struggling to understand how social justice–oriented social studies content could be taught in their schools. They rarely saw social studies taught in their student teaching placements. Seldom, if ever, did my students get to see social justice–oriented social studies modeled for them by their cooperating teachers. If social studies was taught, it was most often taught by the student teachers' cooperating teachers directly from the textbook. Most of my students did not see their cooperating teachers adapting or reforming curriculum to integrate social justice ideals; rather, if social justice issues were discussed in classrooms, the discussion was something separate or compartmentalized from the general curriculum, most often through current events or picture books used in class.

To support my student teachers, I read across multiple multicultural education, social justice–oriented journal articles and books (Au, Bigelow, & Karp, 2007; Bigelow & Peterson, 1998; Christensen, 2009; Cowhey, 2006; Lee, Menkart, & Okazawa-Rey, 2007; Oakes & Lipton, 2007; Sleeter, 2005; Wade, 2007) to document as many strategies as I could find to support them in restructuring and reshaping prescribed curriculum. After documenting the strategies, I looked across the different approaches to see how they might be connected. Once I grouped multiple strategies together, I developed a framework to help teachers strategically navigate curricular structures to plan and enact social justice–oriented social studies curricula.

I used the framework as a scaffold for teaching my students how to build social justice–oriented social studies units, given their curricular constraints. In class I discussed each of the five tenets of the framework and modeled for students what the tenet looked like in practice. I taught a unit consisting of five lesson plans, each lesson plan focusing on a different tenet, beginning with "inspiring wonder" and ending with "facilitating action." After students observed a lesson, we discussed how social studies was integrated with language arts content. At the end of the semester students developed their own units using the framework as their guide and presented the unit to the class. I draw from the student teachers' lessons and my research with beginning teachers (Agarwal, Epstein, Oppenheim, Oyler, & Sonu, 2010; Agarwal, 2012) to provide examples of social justice–oriented social studies lessons. Pseudonyms are used to protect the identities of the students and teachers.

The framework presented in this book is designed to help both novice and experienced teachers in their effort to teach social studies for social justice in a context of language arts. It offers a way of planning that takes into account a variety of factors, including pressures related to content coverage, preparing students for high-stakes tests, and the lack of social studies being taught in our classrooms. In the book I provide an explanation of each tenet of the framework, with strategies to put the framework into practice. Each chapter will explain how you can restructure, reshape, and manipulate mandated curriculum materials to teach from a critical perspective. Given that some teachers may not have many opportunities to teach social studies, I also discuss how you can meet English Language Arts (ELA) Common Core State Standards by teaching language arts and social studies as complementary subjects. This book features examples of classroom practice concretely connected to the language arts Common Core Standards. After each example of classroom practice, you will find the connections to Common Core Standards in text boxes labeled "Connecting to Common Core State Standards." With this feature, you will be able to see how you can meet specific language arts Common Core Standards and enact critical social justice–oriented social studies and language arts curriculum. Through creativity and understanding, it is my belief that we can meet the requirements of our schools, districts, and states and uphold our commitment to teach for social justice.

Acknowledgments

THIS BOOK TOOK form through the help and support of my colleagues, friends, and family. Thank you for your insight, support, and encouragement through this process. I could not have done this without you.

A deep and sincere thank you to Christine Sleeter, my dear friend, mentor, and inspiration. Thank you for opening me to the possibility of writing this book. You shined light on this project in ways that I could never have imagined. Thank you for your continual guidance through each step of the process, including your thorough readings of drafts and your perceptive feedback.

Thank you to Celia Oyler, my long-term adviser and source of encouragement. Thank you for being a beacon of support through the research process and the seeds of this book.

Thank you to Teachers College Press for providing their expertise through each step of the process. Jean Ward, I greatly appreciate your unwavering support and generous ideas for enriching and strengthening the book; your ideas helped to clarify my thinking and strengthen and enrich my writing. A sincere thanks to the anonymous reviewers and the board for their helpful and timely feedback. I am honored to be published by Teachers College Press.

I am deeply grateful to the teachers who contributed to this book. Thank you for inviting me into your classrooms and allowing me to share your work. Your dedication to the profession and your commitment to social justice teaching continue to inspire me each day.

Thank you to my friends and family who offered suggestions and provided support through the writing of this book. Thank you to my parents whose continued love and support has always inspired me to persevere despite any obstacle.

Finally, thank you to my dear partner Praveen Rangnath. You make me believe in the impossible. I am so grateful for your loving support and belief in me through this process. Thank you for pushing me to think critically, move forward, and do what I love to do.

Thank you to our future teachers and readers of this book. I hope that the ideas presented in this book may guide you in your efforts to transform our schools and society to make a better world for all.

CHAPTER 1

Engaging Our Visions

MARIAM LEFT HER teacher education program full of hopes and dreams, believing that she could enact a vision of social justice in her classroom that challenged her students to understand inequity and be social change agents in their school and community. Mariam imagined herself "teaching revolutionaries," and empowering her students to think outside the box about what may be fair or unfair. She envisioned herself creating social awareness among her students and engaging them in discussions around what they could do to make change for themselves and others around them. Even with her high hopes, like many beginning teachers, Mariam found most of her time spent learning how to manage her classroom, prepare students for high-stakes tests, meet standards, and understand the curriculum she was expected to teach. She struggled to translate her visions of social justice into practice given the daily realities of teaching.

Mariam perceived it difficult to teach for social justice because she felt she did not have a clear picture of how to integrate social justice issues into her day-to-day practice as a teacher. As Mariam explained, "I felt like I was ready. I felt like I could do this. But, it was so much harder. Everything was so much harder." Mariam believed she was prepared to teach for social justice after leaving her teacher education program, but the complexity and challenges surrounding her role as a beginning teacher proved differently. As a first-year teacher, Mariam felt she needed help in learning how to navigate standards and the test-driven teaching environment in which she worked. She wished for models of practice where she could learn from other teachers who were successful in both promoting student achievement (as measured by test scores) and also enacting a social justice–oriented social studies curriculum. For Mariam, she felt she had to set aside her commitment to teach for social justice because she was unclear of what social justice teaching looked like in a context of high-stakes testing and standardization. She explained:

> This year was way more than full. I didn't have a clear image. I didn't know when to do it [teach for social justice]. It made me sad . . . I am recognizing it [teaching for social justice] as something much more complex than I thought.

Mariam's story sheds light on the realities of learning to teach for social justice. Learning to teach for social justice is a challenging, complex endeavor. Visionary teachers graduate yearly from social justice–oriented teacher education programs across the United States hoping to work toward a more just and equitable world. Like Mariam, they may envision enacting curriculum that challenges students to critique and examine prevailing social norms, question and think about the world around them, and create change within their schools and communities. Yet, once in the classroom, some teachers may rethink, negotiate, and/or set aside their once-acknowledged commitment to teach for social justice when faced with similar challenges as Mariam, unclear of what teaching for social justice means, unsure of how to translate their vision of social justice teaching into practice, and uncertain of how to integrate social justice ideals into a standards- and test-driven environment. This book is a response to teachers like Mariam, with the intention of helping support their endeavors to teach social studies for social justice with a framework and strategies to maintain a rigorous academic curriculum, meet language arts Common Core Standards, and enrich social studies curriculum to teach from a critical perspective.

This book extends beyond theory and idealism to illustrate and explore ways in which social justice theory can be translated into viable classroom practice. In this book I present a framework to help support teachers in their effort to enact social justice–oriented, literacy-based, social studies curriculum and navigate the tensions between the ideals of teaching for social justice and the realities of classroom practice. The framework is designed to aid in navigating two essential questions:

1. How do we transform and restructure mandated social studies curriculum to teach from a critical, social justice perspective?
2. How do we make room for social studies content when limited to teaching only language arts and math?

The framework consists of five tenets: inspiring wonder, painting the picture, application, connecting the past to the present, and facilitating change (see Figure 1.1).

Each chapter of the book is dedicated to a specific tenet of the framework: It explores one of the tenets, offers concrete strategies to translate the tenet into practice, and relates practical examples of real teachers who are integrating the strategy into their lessons and units. It also discusses ways to teach social studies and literacy as complementary subjects, meet language arts Common Core Standards, and lean on mandated curricular materials to teach from a critical perspective. The examples of teacher practice shared in this book are drawn primarily from K–6 elementary school teachers, yet the framework presented in this book can be used across all disciplines and grade levels. The strategies, examples of teacher practice, and reflection questions

FIGURE 1.1. Social Justice–Oriented Social Studies Framework

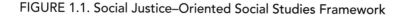

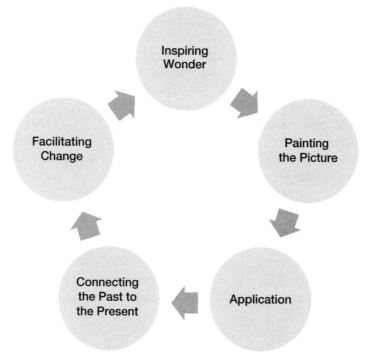

are easily adapted to other grade levels and social studies content. Some of the teachers are represented more than once, showing more than one tenet or strategy in practice, and sometimes specific social studies content like the interactions of indigenous and dominant cultures are shown in more than one teaching example, approached in different ways.

Particular attention is drawn to the second tenet, "painting the picture." This chapter is longer than the others, as this is where students will be delving deeply into critical social studies content. The chapter presents various ways in which teachers are portraying social studies content from multiple perspectives, including simulations, artifact analysis, and using children's literature.

This introductory chapter discusses some of the necessary questions that ground the framework presented in this book: (1) What does it mean to teach for social justice? (2) What is social studies and why don't I see more social studies being taught at my school? (3) How can I integrate literacy, social studies, and social justice? The chapter ends with a discussion of how to best use the framework and strategies presented in this book.

WHAT DOES IT MEAN TO TEACH FOR SOCIAL JUSTICE?

How we think about social justice and what it means to teach for social justice may look different from classroom to classroom, and person to person. The term *social justice* has become a buzzword that can relate to a wide range of different practices and values. For example, some may see teaching for social justice as getting students to get along, while others may see teaching for social justice as an intentional move toward preparing students to be social change agents within their schools and communities. Additionally, some may perceive teaching for social justice as something taught outside of the general curriculum, while others may see teaching for social justice as a vision that translates into everything they do—seating arrangements, lesson plans, conversations with students, and community activity.

Characteristics of social justice teaching that describe what teachers need to know and do in order to enact social justice curriculum in their classrooms include the following:

- Teachers study and learn about the lives of students and their communities.
- Teachers develop and enact academically rigorous curriculum that bolsters learning and achievement of all students in the classroom.
- Teachers challenge students to examine the world around them and encourage students to make change in their schools, communities, and world.
- Teachers see themselves as both responsible for and capable of challenging and altering an educational system that is not adequately serving large numbers of children, particularly poor children, children of color, and children with special needs.
- Teachers work in and around policy constraints to reform and restructure curriculum.

Teaching for social justice from the perspective of this book is a deliberate and intentional effort to know and understand students, manipulate curricular constraints, maintain high expectations for all students, and engage students in a critical pathway of learning. Each of these characteristics are deeply embedded into the framework provided in this book and will be touched upon when discussing each tenet of the framework.

In order to translate social justice into social studies teaching, teachers work to build curriculum that connects to their students' lives and prior learning. Teachers challenge normative thought by integrating multiple perspectives into the curriculum, especially the voices of those dominated, marginalized, or traditionally excluded in texts. Students connect the stories of struggle and resistance to contemporary social justice issues and make connections between historical events and present-day circumstances. In addition, teachers and students work collaboratively to make change in their school and community.

WHAT IS SOCIAL STUDIES AND WHY DON'T I SEE MORE SOCIAL STUDIES BEING TAUGHT AT MY SCHOOL?

Social studies is an interdisciplinary subject area that draws on the concepts, principles, and theories of fields such as anthropology, archaeology, economics, geography, history, law, philosophy, political science, psychology, religion, and sociology. As social studies is about our social world, the content surrounding social studies allows us to investigate people, what they do, and how they interact. The primary purpose of social studies is to help young people develop the ability to make informed and reasoned decisions for the public good as citizens of a culturally diverse, democratic society in an interdependent world (National Council for Social Studies, 2012, p. 3).

As we decide how and when to teach social studies in our classrooms, we make our social studies teaching and learning powerful when we connect social studies content to the lives of our students, give students the opportunity to develop a commitment to social responsibility, justice, and action, draw from the experiences, cultures, and beliefs of the larger social world and its viewpoints, and encourage students to act and participate (Sunal & Haas, 2008).

Social studies is a necessary content area for preparing our students to be critical thinkers and active and informed citizens of our democratic society. In teaching social studies for social justice, teachers can help build students' understandings of our past and present histories while allowing students to examine and take note of unjust actions and inequities in our society. Students can explore multiple perspectives and share their own stories and points of view. Additionally, students can learn from the struggles and resistances of their ancestors and allies to imagine possibilities of social change in their world today. Our history includes a number of movements, changes, and contributions that are the result of the efforts of women, people of color, youth, and other traditionally excluded groups (Darling-Hammond, French, & Garcia-Lopez, 2002). By portraying social studies through the light of multiple cultural viewpoints, we may deepen students' understanding around historical content, provide students with a sense of empowerment that they too can make change in their communities, and find that students are more engaged and involved with the material presented to them.

The challenge with social studies is that attention to its subject matter is often limited or absent from one's daily practice. For example, when one cohort of preservice teachers was asked to raise their hands if they were seeing social studies taught at their school, only half of 32 students raised their hands. Of the 16 students, only 3 were seeing social studies taught every day in their classroom. If social studies was taught it was taught approximately twice a week for 30 minutes.

Subjects assessed in high-stakes testing are the ones most taught in our schools; therefore, social studies is often the most marginalized subject in elementary school curriculum (Cuthrell & Yates, 2007; Wade, 2007). Because literacy and mathematics are assessed in high-stakes standardized tests and deemed as most likely to increase America's domination in the global market (Wade, 2007), little time, resources, and importance are allocated toward social studies instruction. The 60 minutes a week designated for social studies instruction is frequently directly out of a textbook that students find boring, uninteresting, and irrelevant to their daily lives (Loewen, 2007; Wade, 2007).

Yet social studies in its greatest capacity, removed from the confinement and structure of normative thought and uniformed belief, can be a platform for critical thought, investigatory thinking, and social change. At its foundation, social studies is about humanity, examining historical events, people, and places, making connections between the past and the present, studying communities and humanity, countries and our world, deriving meaning in people's social locations and lived experiences, and finding examples in our history of people who are like us, who've fought for us, and have taken significant steps to make the world a better place. Social studies offers a forum for students to discuss critical issues in our past and current histories, to examine and take note of unjust actions and inequities, and to look to the present and future for spaces of possibility and change.

Teaching from the textbook directly, without encouraging students to question and critically think about the messages and assumptions embedded within these texts, may work to perpetuate a harmful story line which negates the experiences, voices, and presence of people whose acts of resistance and contributions have helped build the country we currently live in. As Johnson (2007) explains, traditional curriculum often "denies students the opportunity to benefit from the knowledge, perspectives, and understanding to be gained from studying other cultural groups' experiences and attaining the intercultural competency to work with everyone" (p. 146). We can enrich our social studies teaching by intentionally integrating the history and perspectives of all people. Teaching social studies for social justice might require us to juxtapose historical text and content against various points of reference and multiple perspectives, so that we may be able to develop a more critical and comprehensive understanding of the past and present (Zinn, 2003). In social studies, multiple perspectives are used to analyze issues and ideas through the stories of those who may have been traditionally excluded in texts. The ability to understand multiple viewpoints may allow students to solve complex problems and become more globally aware of the complexity surrounding historical events.

HOW CAN I INTEGRATE LANGUAGE ARTS, SOCIAL STUDIES, AND SOCIAL JUSTICE?

When social studies is not being taught at our schools, we have to think creatively to find space to teach social studies for social justice. Language arts, taught with social studies, is not intended to prepare students for a technical understanding of how to read, write, and speak, "but to empower [children] with multiple perspectives and questioning habits of mind and encourage them to think and take action on their decisions through inquiry, dialogue, activism, and their daily decisions about how to live so that they help make a better world" (Wolk, 2003, p. 102). Teachers help students "read between the lines" (Lee et al., 2007, p. iv), instead of merely reading the lines. By teaching literacy in this way, teachers help their students interrogate the world as a text, counter historical myths, think for themselves, and take action on their decisions through inquiry, dialogue, and activism (Wolk, 2003). In this conception, students are conceived as agents of transformation in classrooms, schools, and communities, raising questions of whose knowledge is in the curriculum, and examining the foundations of history (Au, 2009). This creates the perfect opportunity for students to learn the technical skills they need to pass pencil-and-paper tests and succeed academically (as measured by standardized tests), to read and think in deeply comprehending ways promoted by Common Core State Standards (CCSS), but to also learn to be active members of society.

Integrations Through Read-Alouds

Teachers do not use a read-aloud simply to build reading comprehension in their students, but alternatively use the read-aloud to build a continuous development of issues related to power, inequality, and injustice in human relationships. As Wolk (2003) explains, "Teachers help their students to see and question the dominant power themes in our society and world, such as racism, sexism, corporate and media hegemonies, and the effects on the environment of individuals and systems" (p. 101). By choosing read-alouds that supplement social studies content, a teacher can build students' reading comprehension and fluency while also challenging students to think critically about historical content. By teaching social studies and language arts as complementary subjects, a teacher allows a child's mind to make connections and patterns in learning, building a depth of knowledge and making learning meaningful.

A comprehensive literacy program addresses the essential elements of literacy through research-based teaching methods (Chen & Mora-Flores, 2006). These teaching methods are used strategically and intentionally to help scaffold literacy and language for our learners. Depending on how much time is designated for language arts, teachers may design their comprehensive literacy program accordingly. For example, some teachers may do guided reading groups every day, while others may only have time to do guided reading groups twice a week. Many districts and schools require teachers to have a regimented literacy program that integrates only a few of the methods listed in Table 1.1. As many teachers lean on these methods in their own classrooms, I will return to these methods in subsequent chapters when discussing how social justice–oriented social studies content can be integrated into a language arts period. Table 1.1 briefly describes what each of these methods looks like in the classroom and how the methods could be adapted to integrate language arts and critical social studies content. In this sense, we are upholding a commitment to teach for social justice by developing and enacting academically rigorous curriculum that bolsters achievement of all students in the classroom, while also challenging students to examine the world around them and to think about ways they can make change within their schools and communities.

These methods are grounded in a comprehensive literacy program that is focused on allowing children to fully develop their reading and writing abilities. By teaching language arts and social studies as complementary subjects, a teacher is integrating critical thinking skills and eliciting higher order thinking into subject matter. For example, a teacher may read her fifth-grade students *Sadako and the Thousand Paper Cranes* (Coerr, 1977) as an interactive read-aloud. This is the story of Sadako, a girl who lived in Hiroshima at the time of the atomic bombing by the United States. During guided reading a teacher may continue to integrate social studies and language arts by finding short stories about World War II and the atomic bombing for students to read with their small groups. In guided reading groups a teacher could work on building students' reading comprehension and analytical reading skills, while also getting students to think critically about the perspectives portrayed in their texts. She could ask her students questions such as: Whose voice is heard in the text? Whose is not? How is the message in this text different or the same as Sadako's story? By integrating social studies content into language arts, a teacher is able to cover standards, find space for social studies, and teach students social studies and language arts from a critical perspective.

Pairing with the Common Core Standards

A space in which you can deliberately work to integrate language arts and social studies content is the Common Core Standards, which were developed through a multi-state-led initiative to establish consistent and clear education standards for English language arts and mathematics that better prepare students for college and career readiness and a globally competitive market. As of today, approximately 46 states, the Northern Mariana Islands, and the U.S. Virgin Islands have formally adopted the standards (http://www.corestandards.org/).

TABLE 1.1. Regimented Literacy Program

Method	Description of Method	Critical Perspective
Interactive read-aloud	Teacher reads aloud a book just above students' independent reading level. Teacher provides opportunities for students to ask questions, share ideas, and make connections.	Teacher and students engage in a collaborative construction of meaning. Teacher provides students opportunities to examine texts for bias, misrepresentation, and stereotypes. Teacher builds students' background/content knowledge and awareness. Text connects to students' lived experiences and backgrounds.
Shared reading	Students read together with a teacher. Text is available for students to see and follow. Students learn to read text and make meaning while seeing the text.	Teacher and students engage in a collaborative construction of meaning. Teacher provides students opportunities to examine texts for bias, misrepresentation, and stereotypes. Teacher builds students' background/content knowledge and awareness. Text connects to students' lived experiences and backgrounds.
Independent reading workshop	Students independently read a book they want to read at their independent reading level. While students are reading independently, the teacher can meet with students one-on-one to give them individualized instruction.	Teacher provides students opportunities to examine texts for bias, misrepresentation, and stereotypes. Teacher builds students' background/content knowledge and awareness.
Guided reading	Students read a teacher-selected text in a small group. The teacher provides support and direct teaching.	Teacher and students engage in a collaborative construction of meaning. Teacher provides students opportunities to examine texts for bias, misrepresentation, and stereotypes. Teacher builds students' background/content knowledge and awareness. Text connects to students' lived experiences and backgrounds.
Independent writing workshop	Teacher provides opportunities to help children write independently using the following set of routines: Mini-lesson Independent writing and conferring Partnership talk Whole-group share.	Teacher honors students' voices. Teacher provides students opportunities to write persuasive essays, letters to political leaders, petitions (all opportunities to make change). Method allows for creativity and writing that is grounded in students' lived experiences and backgrounds.
Word study	Students learn about the structure of words and their definitions.	Students build content vocabulary.
Literature circle	Students choose books at their independent reading levels and join reading groups based on their interests.	Teacher and students engage in a collaborative construction of meaning. Teacher provides students opportunities to examine texts for bias, misrepresentation, and stereotypes. Teacher builds students' background/content knowledge and awareness. Text connects to students' lived experiences and backgrounds.

Throughout the book, Common Core Standards are referenced alongside examples of teacher practice. The examples of teacher practice provide us with concrete cases and points of discussion of how we can meet grade-specific English Language Arts Common Core State Standards and teach social justice–oriented social studies lessons. Individual grade-level language arts Common Core State Standards are referenced for specific teachers' lessons in the following categories: Reading: Literature; Reading: Informational Texts; Reading: Foundational Skills; Writing; Speaking and Listening; and Language. In some instances CCR (College and Career Readiness) Anchor Standards, also called Common Core Anchor Standards, are referenced when addressing language arts generally and provide standards in the following areas: Reading, Writing, Speaking and Listening, and Language. Each of these areas lends itself to building and developing students' critical thinking and analytical skills. If we find ways to build bridges between language arts and social studies, we may find greater spaces to teach social studies for social justice, prepare our students to be critical thinkers and learners, and help students meet the particular and complex challenges of reading, writing, speaking, listening, and language.

Language arts and social studies taught as complementary subjects offer the opportunity for social justice issues to emerge from picture books, writing and reading workshops, current events, textbooks, independent reading, and class discussions. Social justice, then, becomes the foundation of the curriculum, instead of something outside or separate. Literacy and social studies, collectively, offer the opportunity for students to engage in meaningful learning that supports students in becoming not only strong, technical readers, but critical, active thinkers as well.

To teach social studies for social justice, we have to think creatively. The marginalization of social studies in our elementary schools, alongside the pressures of covering content and preparing students for standardized tests, does not make it by any means an easy endeavor. This book provides a place to start thinking about how to integrate social studies into daily curriculum. Some readers may work at a school where the study of humanity, diversity in culture and life, and civic duty are honored, but in many more schools teachers need to creatively think of ways to mold social studies into "an already crowded curriculum" (Sleeter, 2005, p. 44).

HOW TO USE THIS BOOK

The framework provided in this book is designed to help teachers navigate mandated curricular constraints to construct social justice–oriented social studies curricula. First, reading the book page by page will help the reader understand how to utilize the overall framework. After reading the book, it can be helpful to reflect in a notebook on the following questions and ideas:

1. How much flexibility do you have? When can you teach social studies? How much do you have to follow a mandated curriculum? When could you integrate social studies into language arts? What standards are you expected to meet? This will help you have a realistic picture of the time you can allot to your social studies curriculum and what you need to do to navigate curricular constraints.
2. Map out your curriculum using your standards or mandated curriculum. What social studies topics do you want to teach? What do you plan not to teach? How long do you have to teach each topic? This will help you decide what to teach and what not to teach and also will allow you to become familiar with the curriculum.
3. Begin with the first topic. Map out the framework (inspiring wonder, painting the picture, application, connecting the past to the present, and facilitating change). Decide what you will teach under each tenet. Think about strategies from the book you can use to help you design your unit. Consider spaces where you can integrate language arts and social studies lessons.
4. Design your lessons. Consider creating a five-lesson unit that follows the framework presented in this book. Use the examples of teacher practice highlighted in the book for ideas and strategies.

SUMMARY OF THE BOOK

It is easy to have high hopes and desire change in this world. It's much more difficult to put that ideal into practice, especially within a context that promotes accountability and standardization. Often the dissonance, or disconnect, we may feel when unable to match actions with beliefs is what leaves us feeling ineffective as teachers. It is my hope that this book provides you with the practical tools you may need in translating a vision of social justice into practice and also a confidence that teaching for social justice is possible. Each chapter will guide you through the framework and share different strategies for use in classrooms. Many examples demonstrate teachers translating each of the tenets into practice, each taking small and significant steps toward disrupting an unjust system and providing a comprehensive, rigorous, and critical curriculum for their students.

Although teachers alone cannot transform society's fundamental inequalities, their work can contribute in many practical ways by raising the social awareness of their students and teaching for social justice (Lalas, 2007). As teachers, we can foster and inspire in students a desire to change what is not right in our schools, communities, and world. We can challenge students to question and think and examine what's unjust and inequitable. And we can work to reform and restructure curriculum so that it is relevant to the needs and experiences of our students and integrates multiple experiences, stories, and narratives.

The purpose of this book is not to move from one prescribed curriculum to another, but to provide a gentle framework in which to support teachers in their efforts to teach for social justice. Each of the subsequent chapters of this book will do the following things: (1) detail one tenet of the framework; (2) ground the tenet in relevant research; (3) discuss strategies that support teachers in integrating the particular tenet of the framework into practice; and (4) share examples of teachers using the tenet in their practice.

Although as teachers we cannot single-handedly change the world, we can take important steps toward bringing about a more just and equitable world. Reforming and restructuring curriculum is an important first step. In these next chapters I discuss how we can begin to transform social studies curriculum to prepare our students to be active, critical, and informed members of society.

CHAPTER 2

Inspiring Wonder

Teaching students to question and think is integral to social justice teaching. Asking questions is what challenges our critical thinkers to examine the world around them so that they may be able to scrutinize and ultimately work to change what may be wrong, unfair, and unjust in our society. While a teacher may be committed to teaching for social justice and preparing her students to be critical thinkers, she or he may struggle to find ways to do this when asked to adhere to a prepackaged, mandated curriculum. Mandated curriculum, when followed directly, often contradicts justice ideals by minimizing opportunities for students to examine historical content through the exploration of multiple perspectives. A justice-oriented curriculum embraces cultural pluralism by honoring the voices and experiences of all members of our society, especially those who are historically silenced and marginalized. Although publishers have addressed some obvious bias in textbooks, researchers have found the experiences and worldviews of Euro-Americans to remain dominant in our structured K–12 history and social studies textbooks (Sleeter, 2011).

By giving students opportunities to question the material in our textbooks, we are allowing our students the chance to be critical thinkers and "raise questions of whose knowledge is in the curriculum and how power and equality are maintained" (Hursh & Ross, 2000, p. 10). An essential aspect of social justice education is to challenge students to think critically about the material presented to them, so that they may, in Ira Shor's words, "see knowledge as a field of contending interpretations" (1992, p. 15). Shor provides the following questions for us to think about when examining texts for knowledge and power:

- Whose literature and history is taught and whose is ignored?
- Which groups are included and which are left out?
- From whose point of view is the past and present represented?

When we use questions like these to challenge our students to think about knowledge and power, we offer our children the opportunity to question social reality and think critically about the underlying values and assumptions embedded within the texts surrounding us. Through this critical thinking, students develop their capacity to question, critique, and challenge what may

13

seem unfair or unjust. For example, students may watch a Disney movie and be able to see the gender roles and stereotypes assigned to characters in the film. They may read about Christopher Columbus and examine from whose perspective the story is told. Or watching a commercial on television, they may think about how the advertisement perpetuates stereotypes, targets specific groups, or influences normative thinking.

In preparing our critical thinkers, inspiring wonder is integral to getting our students to question and think about the world they live in and the injustices that surround them. Wonder, in this light, sets the stage for intrigue, surprise, question, uncertainty, and inquiry. Inspiring wonder is the first tenet of the framework developed in this book, as wonder is often what awakens and motivates students to connect to subject matter. In providing opportunities for discovery and surprise, students are constructing their own knowledge and "feeling powered and energized enough to go further in their expectations of the world and their own minds" (Ayers, 2001, p. 91). This way, students are offered a glimpse so intriguing that they are left wondering, "What's next?" Curiosity, intrigue, and wonder allow knowledge to be socially constructed, based on what a student has experienced, knows, and is interested in.

This chapter discusses how to inspire wonder in students and create a starting point from which to teach a social studies unit through a social justice lens. It will unpack what it means to inspire wonder, discuss strategies to inspire wonder with examples of teacher practice, examine ways in which social studies content can be connected to language arts, and discuss how teachers may navigate mandated curricular materials and accountability structures to find space to integrate the strategies discussed in this chapter. It will also highlight ways in which the language arts Common Core Standards can be used as a bridge to integrate social studies content into language arts. As inspiring wonder is the first tenet of this framework, the strategies listed in this chapter are designed to help teachers begin a social studies unit or lesson. However, each of these strategies can be used throughout a social studies lesson or unit at any time. By inspiring wonder in students, we are providing opportunities for them to be critical thinkers and experience learning that is connected to their prior knowledge and lived experiences.

BUILDING ON STUDENTS' PRIOR KNOWLEDGE

Inspiring wonder in students, in relation to the lesson being taught, cannot be merely produced by asking an intriguing question or developing a creative simulation. To facilitate curiosity and wonder, we must think about our students, specifically their interests and experiences, the questions they may have, and their prior learning in order to develop questions and activities that they may connect to (Ayers, 2001; Gonzalez, Moll, & Amanti, 2005; Ladson-Billings, 1994). Making explicit connections between new learning and the materials, vocabulary, and concepts previously covered in class is an essential piece to building students' background knowledge (Echeverria, Vogt, & Short, 2004).

Wonder engages children's minds and sets the stage of learning in two ways: a desire to activate an existing knowledge, and a wish for exploring and obtaining new information. Children lean on their memories to activate a knowledge base from which to derive information. In learning about Christopher Columbus, for example, a student may make the connection that her parent also traveled from Europe to America in search of a better life. Another student may remember his teacher reading a book to the class about Christopher Columbus. This background knowledge base not only offers a teacher the opportunity to build off what students know, but also the chance to challenge students' misconceptions and further their critical understandings of historical stories. Wonder, then, emerges from students' curiosity about the world and their desire to understand why.

Bridging to New Learning

Prior to engaging in facilitating activities and discussions that evoke wonder in students, it is integral that we first build on students' interests, experiences, and prior learning—building a bridge from previous lessons to new learning for students to cross over. This can be done by setting up the beginning of the lesson or unit in the following way:

- Activate background knowledge
- State objective (connecting prior learning to new learning)
- Awaken students' questions
- Preteach vocabulary
- Use an activity to inspire wonder

By setting up the lesson in this way, one can assess what students want to learn and invite their questions, while also making clear what the objectives of the lesson are and the key vocabulary students need to know. Introducing key vocabulary can meet some of the Common Core Anchor Standards for Language. For example, a teacher may introduce the word *segregation* during a unit on the Civil War. She may teach her third graders how to use context clues in the sentence to uncover what the word *segregation* might mean. As this teacher is not merely giving her students a vocabulary word and definition, but engaging her students in an initiated word study, a teacher can meet the following Common Core Anchor Standards for Language:

> **Connecting to Common Core State Standards**
>
> *Vocabulary Acquisition and Use*
>
> Determine or clarify the meaning of unknown and multiple-meaning words and phrases by using context clues, analyzing meaningful word parts, and consulting general and specialized reference materials, as appropriate.

Mariel's Classroom—Discrimination During the Gold Rush

By highlighting and unpacking key vocabulary prior and during a social studies lesson, we can build background knowledge for students and address key Common Core Standards. In this next passage, Mariel's lesson will serve as an example of how to inspire wonder in students in the first lesson of a unit, using the suggestions listed above. In this example, Mariel activates background knowledge, states her objective, awakens students' questions, pre-teaches vocabulary, and then engages students in an activity to inspire wonder.

Mariel teaches fourth grade in Oakland, California. The objective of her lesson is to teach students about the discrimination against the Chinese during the Gold Rush period. To connect prior learning to new concepts, she asks her students these questions: "What do you know about immigration? Do you know anyone who immigrated to the United States? Why do you think they left their families and loved ones to come to the United States?" Mariel jots students' responses on a KWLQ chart at the front of her room (K: What you know, W: What you wonder about, L: What you learned, Q: What questions you still have). She then asks her students, "Who remembers what we learned last week?"

After students share their responses, Mariel writes the objective of the lesson on the board and explains, "Last week we discussed the Gold Rush and the large-scale immigration of the Chinese to California during this time. Today we are going to look critically at the Chinese Exclusion Act, which restricted Chinese immigration to the United States." After stating the objective, Mariel asks her students to share what they may be wondering about, in pairs: "What do you think the Chinese Exclusion Act is about? How do you think the Chinese were treated about this time? What questions do you have? What are you wondering about?" After students respond to their partners, Mariel asks them to share with the class. Mariel records her students' responses on a KWLQ chart, under the letter W. She then explains to students that they will be exploring their questions through the unit.

As Mariel is limited to 30 minutes of social studies time twice a week, Mariel continues the lesson during her language arts period the next morning. Mariel is required to teach 120 minutes of language arts each day. Part of her language arts instructional period is dedicated to word study. Often, Mariel uses this time to build content area vocabulary and preteach essential words to her students. In this case, Mariel wants her students to learn the words: *detain, justice,* and *exclusion*. The words are listed on the board, accompanied by a picture and the definition. To preteach vocabulary, Mariel walks students through each word, describing what it means, while also showing them pictures that illustrate the word. Mariel also reviews words she has used in previous lessons that are relevant to this lesson as well. The words, pictures, and definitions are left on the board for students to use as a resource throughout the social studies unit. Through Mariel's preteaching strategies, she is able to cover the following English Language Arts (ELA) Common Core Standards for Language, grade 4:

Connecting to Common Core State Standards

Vocabulary Acquisition and Use

L.4.4.   Determine or clarify the meaning of unknown and multiple-meaning words and phrases based on grade 4 reading and content, choosing flexibly from a range of strategies.

After preteaching vocabulary, Mariel continues to use her language arts period to integrate social studies concepts. She uses the time she normally devotes to shared reading to read the following poem (Lai, Lim, & Yung, 1991) with her students. The poem is written on chart paper so students have access to the words:

America has power, but not justice.
In prison, we were victimized as if we were guilty.
Given no opportunity to explain, it was really brutal.
I bow my head in reflection but there is
nothing I can do.

After reading the poem with her class, Mariel asks her students questions such as, "Who do you think wrote this poem? Why do you think this poem was written? What do you think this poem means?" Through Mariel's shared reading and discussion of the text with her students, Mariel could meet the following ELA Common Core Standards for Reading: Literature, grade 4:

Connecting to Common Core State Standards

Key Ideas and Details

RL.4.1. Refer to details and examples in a text when explaining what the text says explicitly and when drawing inferences from the text.

Table 2.1. KWLQ Chart

K	W	L	Q
What do you know?	What do you want to learn?	What did you learn?	What questions do you still have?

By engaging her students in a discussion around the text and asking students to infer who the poem might be written by, Mariel is able to meet Common Core Standards for reading. Mariel closes the lesson by reviewing the key vocabulary and asking students what they learned today. Mariel then explains to students that they will be "painting the picture" tomorrow, further discussing and looking at the Chinese Exclusion Act from the perspective of the Chinese.

In this example, Mariel carefully constructs new learning with her students. She not only connects new content to students' experiences and prior learning, but also highlights and unpacks important vocabulary. Mariel chose select words she perceived as critical for understanding the text or material and provided a variety of ways for her students to develop their content vocabulary (Echeverria & Graves, 2007). She also awakened students' questions by asking them what they might know about the Chinese Exclusion Act and how the Chinese people were treated during this time. After building students' background knowledge, she then attempts to inspire awareness and wonder in her students by reading a poem written by the Chinese detainee. This launching point becomes the beginning of a lesson or unit, where she can then guide students into a deeper examination of the Chinese Exclusion Act.

While limited with the time she was able to teach social studies, Mariel creatively integrated social studies content into her language arts period. In this way, Mariel was able to uphold her commitment to teach social studies for social justice, while also finding ways to maintain her comprehensive literacy program and meet language arts Common Core Standards.

The next section details strategies that may be used as the poem was used by Mariel to heighten students' sense of awareness and wonder. The strategies work well at the beginning of a lesson or unit, but can also be integrated throughout any lesson. The purpose of the strategies is to build students' curiosity about a theme, idea, or topic and to get students critically thinking about what happened and why.

AWAKENING STUDENTS' QUESTIONS

Children are curious by nature. They wonder about ideas like why the sky is blue and why trees are green. Young children ask "why" questions all the time. As Levstik and Barton (2005) assert, "children are naturally inquisitive learners who strive to make sense of their world (p. 19)." Although children are innately curious, in school they often learn not to ask questions. As young as age 7, students feel the pressure of having to choose an answer on a multiple-choice test without ever having to question it. In this sense, their desire to wonder and be curious may be squashed. There is an implicit message in many classrooms and schools for students to remain quiet, learn what they need to learn, and pass the test. Consequently, students learn not to ask questions in schools and not to question what they learn in school. In a social justice classroom, however, students are encouraged to use their voices and share their opinions so that they are active, contributing members of their classroom community. Teachers can take advantage of students' curiosity and wonder by allowing opportunities for students to explore their important and meaningful questions.

We need to awaken and invite the questions children do have. To tap into wonder and the questions students bring to a new topic, concept, idea, or theme, a KWL (Ogle, 1986) or KWLQ chart or graphic organizer (Schmidt, 1999) is a quick way for teachers to learn what students are wondering about and to build on their prior learning. We saw Mariel do this in her lesson on the Chinese Exclusion Act. In a KWLQ, the teachers have a big piece of chart paper on the front board. The chart paper is divided into four columns. Each column represents a different letter (see Table 2.1).

Teachers often use a KWLQ graphic organizer to begin a new unit. At the beginning of a unit, a teacher has her students fill out the K and W of the chart. Normally students share their answers and the teacher records their answers on the board. Sometimes students have their own KWLQ chart that they fill out individually or in groups. The purpose of doing the graphic organizer collaboratively is so that students can learn from each other. The K in the graphic organizer is to assess and elicit students' prior learning. The W is to document their burning questions. In documenting students' burning questions, we can create lessons that connect directly to what they are interested in learning about.

KWLQ charts can be written or drawn. Students could draw to show what they know or have learned about particular social studies content. This may support English language learners in the classroom who may be better able to articulate themselves through drawings than written language.

KWLQ charts allow you to elicit and build on the questions students have. By awakening students' wonder in this way, they will be more excited about what they are learning and therefore be more likely to connect to the content. A teacher could also integrate literacy into this social studies lesson by reinforcing key vocabulary during the KWLQ discussion. By explicitly teaching and reinforcing key vocabulary through developmentally appropriate strategies such as using context clues, a teacher can meet grade-level vocabulary acquisition and use language arts Common Core Standards. A KWLQ is a quick way to both assess students' prior learning and awaken students' questions about the topic being introduced to them. Through a KWLQ activity, a teacher can also meet Common Core Anchor Standards for Speaking and Listening:

Connecting to Common Core State Standards

Comprehension and Collaboration

Prepare for and participate effectively in a range of conversations and collaborations with diverse partners, building on others' ideas and expressing their own clearly and persuasively.

Because students are engaged in a collaborative discussion either with partners, in groups, or as a whole class, teachers can meet Common Core Standards for speaking and listening because they are deliberately providing a space for students to express and share their ideas with one another. A teacher's effort to include a KWLQ into a social studies unit can inspire wonder, assess students' prior knowledge, offer opportunities for students to better engage with the social studies content, and encourage students to consider "what's next?"

ARTIFACT ANALYSIS

In an artifact analysis students examine documents for inconsistencies, biases, misconceptions, and inaccuracies. Artifacts might include primary sources such as photographs, websites, letters, legal transcripts, or illustrations by someone who was there. Schmidt (2007) explains that primary sources help you get as close as possible to what actually happened, "as they are artifacts of a certain time, created at the time being studied, by the people being studied" (p. 47). Primary sources give you an authentic starting place from which to launch a critical exploration into the past. Many primary artifacts can be found in social studies textbooks. When preparing to teach a unit or lesson, it is a good idea to thumb through the textbook for documents or photographs that may facilitate students' critical thinking.

The purpose of the artifact analysis is for students to wonder and think about what is presented before them. Artifact analysis, in this sense, is used to inspire wonder: Who is that person in the picture? Why are they happy, sad, or angry? An analysis of a document can also be used to challenge students to think critically: Whose perspective is this document written from? Whose voice is visible? Whose is not? Who benefits from this document? Who may be harmed by this document? The artifact analysis strategy can be used at the beginning of a lesson or unit to spark curiosity in students, motivating students to wonder and think critically about the person, theme, idea, or event being introduced to them.

When integrating language arts and social studies, artifact analysis can be used with interactive read-alouds. For example, many nonfiction read-alouds have pictures and documents that are great to analyze from a critical perspective. In this vein, students are both building comprehension and learning to think critically about the texts presented to them. A teacher could also use an interactive read-aloud to read and discuss important documents such as the Constitution or Bill of Rights. During the read-aloud a teacher reads the document to students and has a copy of the document available for students to see. The teacher might ask students questions such as:

- What is the purpose of the document?
- Who stands to benefit from the document? Who stands to be hurt from the document?
- How has this written document affected your rights?
- What would you change?

Using the interactive read-aloud method in this way allows a teacher to reinforce important content vocabulary, collaboratively group students during the reading to build comprehension and understanding of the text, model important reading comprehension strategies, and challenge students to think critically about the documents being presented to them. With this in mind, a teacher could potentially meet the following language arts Common Core Anchor Standards for Reading (see page 22).

Each of these standards could be broken down and taught, while engaging students in a document analysis. For example, a teacher could have students look critically at the text to determine whose perspective may be included or not included in the document. Through this activity, a teacher could explicitly teach students how point of view and purpose shape a text and its content.

Teaching literacy and social studies as complementary subjects can creatively make space for social studies teaching when constraints of time make teaching social studies in isolation difficult. Being conscious of how we can meet Common Core Standards in language arts through the integration of

> ### Connecting to Common Core State Standards
>
> *Key Ideas and Details*
>
> Read closely to determine what the text says explicitly and to make logical inferences from it; cite specific textual evidence when writing or speaking to support conclusions drawn from the text.
>
> Determine central ideas or themes of a text and analyze their development; summarize the key supporting details and ideas.
>
> *Craft and Structure*
>
> Assess how point of view or purpose shapes the content and style of a text.

social studies and language arts allows for crossover between subject areas, which makes learning more meaningful for students.

Sarah's Classroom—Native Americans

Sarah, a third-grade teacher in Oakland, opened her five-lesson unit on the Ohlone people using the strategy of artifact analysis. The Ohlone people are Native Americans who have lived in the San Francisco Bay area for centuries.

To begin, Sarah shows a photograph of an elderly Ohlone woman (photographed in the 1920s) on the overhead projector. Sarah asks her students, "What do you notice in the photograph? Who do you think this a portrait of? Have you heard of the Ohlone people? What do you know about them?" As students share, Sarah records their responses on the front board. After the discussion, Sarah explains that the photograph is of Isabelle Meadows, a Native American woman from the Ohlone tribe. Next to the photograph is the word *Ohlone* with a definition available for students to reference.

After sharing information about Isabelle Meadows, Sarah shows a photograph of John P. Harrington, an anthropologist who studied the Ohlone people. Sarah explains that Isabelle Meadows and John P. Harrington contributed greatly to the documentation of the Ohlone culture, history, language, and folklore. After introducing both photographs, Sarah states the objective of the lesson: "Today we are going to become anthropologists and learn about the history and culture of a civilization that once flourished where we now live."

Artifact analysis, in this example, was used at the beginning of Sarah's unit on the Ohlone people to spark students' critical thinking and draw on students' prior learning. In later lessons, Sarah has her students listen to creation myths and learn about how the Ohlone culture has survived despite the treatment of the people and their land, engage in independent research projects, read materials from the perspective of the Ohlone people, evaluate images of the colonists and Native Americans in conflict, and write letters to the colonists from the perspective of the Ohlone people, advocating for their rights.

Language Arts Approach

If limited with time, we can easily translate the activity enacted by Sarah into a language arts period. For example, Sarah could begin the lesson introducing key content vocabulary. The vocabulary work is then part of her word study time. The key vocabulary could be shared through pictures, definitions, Total Physical Response method (Asher, 1969), and/or word walls. After Sarah shared the content vocabulary with her students, she could post the words and pictures on a bulletin board or word wall for students to use as a resource through the unit. By unpacking important content vocabulary and teaching strategies to students that help develop vocabulary (e.g., using context clues, learning suffixes and affixes), Sarah could cover the following ELA Common Core Standard for Language, grade 3:

Connecting to Common Core State Standards

Vocabulary Acquisition and Use

L.3.4.   Determine or clarify the meaning of unknown and multiple-meaning words and phrases based on grade 3 reading and content, choosing flexibly from a range of strategies.

When giving students explicit teaching around key content vocabulary, Sarah is making content more accessible to all of her students, especially English language learners, and also meeting language arts Common Core Standards for Language. While teaching vocabulary, Sarah could provide students with strategies to help them determine the meaning of unknown words. Teaching strategies such as context clues and root words will help enhance students' language development.

After introducing vocabulary, Sarah could then project the picture of Isabelle Meadows and introduce the idea of "prediction." Prediction, a key reading comprehension strategy, allows students to generate questions based on what students already know about the topic or idea they're learning about. Tompkins (2010) reminds us that "comprehension strategies are thoughtful behaviors that students use to facilitate their understandings as they read" (p. 260).

When students learn to make predictions, they learn to make claims and interpretations based on evidence collected from texts, discussions, and lived experiences. For example, in Sarah's classroom, students could use details from the picture of Isabelle Meadows and their prior knowledge to make predictions of who she may be and what they may be learning about.

When teachers are asked to directly follow a mandated curriculum, artifact analysis is a great strategy to use in order to get students to think critically about the text. Most of our textbooks have many great primary resources such as letters, pictures, and documents. Students can be directed to read a passage of their textbooks to build background, then look critically at the picture/document that accompanies the text and consider the following questions:

- Does the picture/document relay the same message as the text?
- Whose voice/face is missing from the picture or document? Whose voice/face is heard/visible?
- Who does this picture or document harm? Who does it benefit?
- Why do you think this picture was taken? Why do you think this document was written?

Teachers with limited time or space to teach social studies for social justice have to be creative. Even when expected to adhere to a mandated curriculum, one can pose questions to students along the way to get them thinking critically about what they are reading. In this way, students not only learn to comprehend the text, but also learn to question and think about what is presented to them. By collapsing social studies content into a comprehensive literacy program, Sarah is intentionally teaching language arts and social studies as complementary subjects and meeting language arts Common Core Standards.

GUIDING SIMULATION

Guided simulations help students understand and relate to people and events from another time or place (Wade, 2007). In this imaginary replication, students become figures in history, engaging in events that may allow them to connect to the lives of historical figures and feel emotions from another's perspective. Thus simulation becomes a metaphor for the authentic engagements in the past that we cannot experience. Carmen Ozick (1989) elaborates on the metaphor:

> Through metaphor, the past has the capacity to imagine us, and we it. Through metaphorical concentration, doctors can imagine what it is to be their patients. Those who have not pain can imagine those who suffer. Those at the center can imagine what it is to be outside. The strong can imagine the weak. Illuminated caves can imagine the dark. Poets in their twilight can imagine the borders of stellar fire. We strangers can imagine the familiar hearts of strangers. (p. 283)

Metaphor or simulation allows us to imagine what it was like for people in a specific moment in time. Levstik and Barton (2005) suggest that through imaginative entries we may "recognize that no society or group of people is wholly wise or virtuous, that all of us have the capacity for both good and ill" (p. 88). In this sense, guiding simulations offer students the opportunity to enter into a moment in history, to see historical events from multiple perspectives, and to find empathy across a range of human experience. Feelings such as anger, fear, sadness, hurt, or happiness may surface in simulations and/or follow-up discussions. Acting out historical stories in the classroom can bring history to life in powerful and moving ways (Kornfeld & Leyden, 2005). By developing simulations, teachers can help students examine history from multiple perspectives, challenging them to think about issues such as colonization, oppression, power, and privilege.

While simulations can work to replicate historical events, simulations can also work to resemble or parallel an idea, theme, or concept.

Carmen's Classroom—Discrimination

Carmen uses simulation in her third-grade classroom in Oakland, California, to represent the notion of discrimination. To begin with, Carmen tells students that they will be drawing what they want to be on a piece of paper. She then divides the students into two groups, those taller than 4 feet and those shorter than 4 feet. She states, "If you're shorter than 4 feet, here are your materials." The teacher shows students several bins of nicely arranged, high-quality materials, including special materials that the students do not normally use. The teacher then shows the students above 4 feet, several bins of poor-quality materials (broken crayons, stubby pencils, and so on).

Carmen reminds students that she has decided this, and that no one may take other materials aside from the ones given to them by the teacher. Carmen also tells the students that those shorter than 4 feet will be allowed to drink water while they work, but those taller than 4 feet will not be allowed to drink water until after recess. After students work for approximately 10 minutes, the teacher stops students to discuss feelings that arose for them during the simulations. She asks:

- How did that feel?
- How did you feel about me as your teacher when you heard my rules?
- If you were taller than 4 feet, how did you feel when I showed you the different materials?
- If you were shorter than 4 feet, how did you feel?
- Was what I did fair? Why? Or why not?

Through the imaginary replication, students were able to experience discrimination and feel emotions such as pain, anger, guilt, and hurt. During the activity, students struggled about being in either group, those privileged or discriminated against. The students who felt privileged felt bad for having better supplies, while the students discriminated against felt angry for not having good materials to work with. The negative feelings that emerged from the simulation offered Carmen the perfect segue into a conversation about discrimination. In subsequent lessons, students engaged in a critical analysis of discrimination and segregation laws enacted between 1876 and 1965 and nonviolent methods of protest, including Nelson Mandela's fight for Black rights in South Africa.

In this example, simulation was used to introduce a concept and deepen students' understandings around a particular idea, theme, or notion. In Carmen's case, she wanted her students to understand the concepts of privilege and discrimination. The purpose of the simulation was to challenge students to critically think about important social justice concepts, while inspiring a sense of wonder and curiosity to propel them into subsequent lessons.

Jean's Classroom—Forced Relocation

Jean is a fifth-grade teacher in San Francisco, California. Students have been read aloud *Soft Rain* by Cornelia Cornelissen (1998) as an introduction to a unit on Native Americans and their forced removal from their homelands. Told from the perspective of a 9-year-old girl of the Cherokee nation, *Soft Rain* traces the events that led to the forced relocation of an entire Native American tribe from the southeastern United States to designated tribal lands in Oklahoma in 1838.

The purpose of the simulation is to introduce a unit on the removal and relocation of Native American nations in 1838. Due to Andrew Jackson's policy, Native Americans were forced to give up their lands east of the Mississippi River and migrate to an area in present day Oklahoma. In route, many Native Americans suffered and died from illness and starvation due to weather conditions, lack of food, and exposure to outside diseases.

Students sit quietly at their desks while Jean relays the objective and activities for the day. Jean states: "Our goal is to continue to learn about the Trail of Tears and how it contributes to the theme of conflict between Native Americans and European settlers, and how we could respond to this conflict today. We will do this by participating in a guided simulation, followed by a read-aloud of a nonfiction text."

Jean begins reading students a fake letter, telling students that this letter was written by a fifth-grade class from a different school. In the letter, their teacher says that her fifth-grade class from Wildwood Elementary has hereby decided that they don't want to continue learning in their current fifth-grade classroom. They are tired of their principal not giving them freedom on the play yard and in the halls. They want to explore new classrooms where they could change these rules, and they have chosen ours. They will be arriving 2 days from now and are expecting all of us to leave by then. Because they don't want us to be without a classroom, however, they have allowed us to take all our belongings that we can carry and move into that fourth-grade classroom on the first floor. Even though there are already students there, they figure we can share it. The letter is signed by the fifth-grade teacher, Ms. So-and-So.

After reading the letter, Jean prompts questions to her class such as these: What do you think about this letter? How would you respond to it? How should we respond as a class? What should we tell the fourth-grade class whose classroom we are supposed to share? Who can we turn to for help? Jean alternates between partner sharing and calling on hands. The simulation ends by Jean telling students that they will continue to process this and compare the simulation to real historical events.

In subsequent lessons Jean continues to paint a picture of what happened during the Indian Removal Act by reading them a nonfiction children's book about the Trail of Tears and engaging students in a second simulation where students are divided into three groups: Black Seminoles, Cherokees, and the American Government. This simulation will be detailed in the next chapter.

Here, Jean draws concrete connections between literacy and social studies. Prior to introducing a social studies unit on Native Americans, she deliberately chooses to read her students a book during language arts that helps build their background knowledge about the experiences of Native Americans because of the Indian Removal Act. When stating her objective at the start of the lesson, she makes the connection between prior learning and new learning explicit for her students. She then offers students the opportunity to engage in a simulation which allows them to emulate the experiences of the Native Americans. Jean guides a simulation to make learning real and accessible to her students, while also inspiring curiosity in her students about what's next. Students are not passively receiving information, but get to be an active part of the process.

The simulations described above offer students the opportunity to step into history and experience some of the decision making and unscripted possibilities that real people in history may have also experienced. Students can also see the paths of struggle and resistance faced by groups and people who are often underrepresented or glossed over in textbooks. Imaginative entry allows students to be characters in history. Through encounters, students may gain deeper understandings of oppression, power, and privilege, inspiring in them a sense of injustice and a hope for change.

In terms of teaching social studies and language arts as complementary subjects, simulations make this integration more challenging yet possible. In using simulations in the classroom to inspire wonder, teachers can meet the Common Core Anchor Standards for Speaking and Listening on page 28.

> **Connecting to Common Core State Standards**
>
> *Comprehension and Collaboration*
>
> Prepare for and participate effectively in a range of conversations and col-laborations with diverse partners, building on others' ideas and expressing their own clearly and persuasively.

To enact a simulation in the classroom and meet language arts Common Core Anchor Standards for Speaking and Listening, a teacher needs to pro-vide opportunities for students to share ideas, collaborate, and discuss their beliefs both during and after the simulation. For example, after the simulation a teacher could engage students in a collaborative discussion asking students critical questions about the simulation such as: What did it feel like to par-ticipate in the simulation? Who had power? Who did not have power? Whose perspective did we get to see? Whose perspective did we not get to see? Ask-ing critical questions after a simulation provides teachers with opportunities to teach social justice–oriented lessons and meet language arts Common Core Standards for speaking and listening.

PERSONAL STORIES

Learning history, particularly stories of struggle and resistance, is often most powerfully understood through the words of those who experienced the his-torical events themselves. These stories can be found in interviews and histori-cal documents, such as newspapers, letters, poems, and diaries; other times we can look to community members for stories that may convey struggle and resistance. Stories of ourselves can be most powerful, as they show our strug-gles, our capacity to fail and stand up, and our fragility as human beings. In this sense, our understanding of humanity and compassion develops as much from stories about human failure as from stories of triumph. In short, stories of struggle and resistance allow us to see our points of intersection, where we hope to be validated, recognized, or victorious. Personal stories shared at the beginning of a lesson or unit can be a great way to draw our learners in and introduce a concept, idea, or historical event.

Claire's Classroom—Farmworkers Movement

Claire is a third-grade teacher in Oakland, California. The objective of her lesson is to teach students about the Farmworkers Movement in 1965.

To begin her lesson, Claire shares her struggle of being a teacher in Oakland. She explains how she and her fellow teachers gathered together in the spring of 2010 to protest teachers' salaries and class-size increases. She explains to her students what a strike is and how she and her colleagues organized the strike. After sharing her story, she introduces the idea of discrimination and protest. She then asks her third-grade students, "Have you ever heard of the Farmworkers Movement? What do you know about the struggle the farmworkers faced?" After eliciting students' prior knowledge, Claire discusses with her students the treatment of farmworkers and shows students slides of farmworkers protesting the conditions through marches, strikes, and boycotts during the United Farmworkers Movement. She continues with a series of five lessons, ending with an activity that asks students to find ways they could peacefully protest a struggle that they were affected by within their school and community.

In Claire's classroom, a storied experience was used as a setting to introduce social studies content. Claire linked her own struggle as a teacher protesting to the social studies content being presented. Also, Claire used her storied experience to introduce the idea of protest and build students' background knowledge.

Personal stories from historical figures, community members, or ourselves can be significant ways of exploring struggle and resistance both in the past and the present. Storied experiences can serve as models of how to make change individually and collectively, inspiring solidarity and activism among ourselves and our students.

Language Arts Approach

Personal stories can be a great place to integrate literacy and social studies. For example, a story of resistance and struggle could be used for a shared reading activity. *Shared reading*, a driving force underlying a balanced literacy program, is "a collaborative learning experience in which students read with the teacher as she navigates them through the text" (Chen & Mora-Flores, 2006, p. 65). In shared reading, students are provided with visible access to the texts either through an enlarged text, such as big books and charts, or individual copies. Using the text, teachers think out loud to students, modeling how to decode and make sense of the text. In social justice teaching, a teacher not only models effective reading strategies but also demonstrates to students how to engage with a text from a critical perspective, questioning themes that may arise such as gender roles, oppression, and discrimination. The repeated exposure to the text widens and deepens students' experiences with new vocabulary and builds students' oral language (Chen & Mora-Flores, 2006). Often, shared reading is only used in primary grades to teach students about concepts of print, but I believe shared reading could also be used as an important teaching method for upper grades as well to model both critical thinking and reading comprehension strategies.

Personal stories, if in a written format, can also be used as interactive read-alouds. When choosing a read-aloud, choose a book just above a reader's independent reading level. This allows students to access information they may not be able to understand on their own. Teachers may begin the reading by front-loading vocabulary, making the text accessible to all learners in the classroom, especially the English language learners. When front-loading vocabulary, the teacher is intentionally teaching key vocabulary prior to reading a story. As Chen and Mora-Flores (2006) note, "Front-loading vocabulary is not giving a vocabulary lesson; it is just presenting students with a simple definition of the word to enhance comprehension of the story" (p. 37). By preteaching vocabulary, the teacher offers students the opportunity to gain a better understanding of the text because they have already been exposed to some of the key words in the story through pictures or oral definitions.

During the read-aloud, a teacher may stop to scaffold and deepen students' understanding of the text by asking questions that challenge students to think critically about the historical context of the storied account:

- Why was the personal account written?
- For whom is the text written?
- Who stands to benefit from or be hurt by the text?
- How is language used in specific ways to convey the author's message?
- What emotions are grounded in the author's message?
- Can you relate to what the author is saying?

Teachers can stop the reading to ask students critical questions about the text in a whole group, or they can have students share their answers to discussion questions in pairs or small groups. The purpose of the read-aloud is to spark students' curiosity about a historical event or occurrence and to get them thinking critically about what happened, why it happened, and who benefited from what happened.

By presenting a personal story either through a shared reading or interactive read-aloud, a teacher could potentially meet the following Common Core Anchor Standards for Reading on the next page.

While engaging students in a shared reading or interactive read-aloud, a teacher needs to ask students critical questions about the text to offer them opportunities to make inferences, determine central ideas and themes, and analyze character development. Questions such as, "Why do you think the character felt this way?" or "What do you think the character should do?" may help students think critically about the personal story. It is also always helpful for students if their teacher models strategies such as making inferences so that students are clear about what this means. Explicitly teaching strategies such as

---

Connecting to Common Core State Standards

Key Ideas and Details

Read closely to determine what the text says explicitly and to make logical inferences from it; cite specific textual evidence when writing or speaking to support conclusions drawn from the text.

Determine central ideas or themes of a text and analyze their development; summarize the key supporting details and ideas.

---

determining central ideas or summarizing through a personal story can enact a social justice–oriented social studies lesson in the classroom and meet language arts Common Core Standards.

CONNECTING NEW LEARNING TO STUDENTS' EXPERIENCES, INTERESTS, AND BACKGROUND KNOWLEDGE

Teachers ask students questions for different reasons, such as to build reading comprehension, check for understanding, or challenge students to think outside the box. In social justice education, asking questions is an essential element, initiating critical thinking and social activism. Asking questions is what grounds our critical thinkers and forces them to question singular ways of thinking. Moreover, questioning provides a powerful launching pad for discussions into the complexities associated with issues of racism, sexism, class, oppression, and other forms of inequality. In teaching social studies for social justice, "students learn how to develop questions and gather information in ways that enable them not only to better understand society, but also to change it" (Au, 2009, p. 26). In this regard, critical curriculum challenges status quo norms of historical knowledge. As teachers, we can ask critical questions to our students, offering students the opportunity to question texts, historical events, and opinions of others, or to connect relevant background knowledge to a new lesson.

To instill wonder, often teachers use a questioning approach to connect content to students' lived experiences. Echevarria and Graves (2007) assert that "tapping into existing knowledge will involve asking students to generate questions or tell what they know prior to studying a unit or chapter" (p. 84). Using connections from the lives of students serves the dual purpose of linking new knowledge to existing knowledge and validating students' lived experiences (Echevarria & Graves, 2007). In this sense, learning is situated in students' everyday existence, thus helping them to understand its relevancy (Wolk, 2003).

Tanya's Classroom—Rosa Parks and Ruby Bridges

Tanya is a third-grade teacher in Oakland. The objective of her lesson is for students to understand Rosa Parks's contributions, the context in which they occurred, and how they affect us today.

To begin her lesson, Tanya asks her students to think about the following question with their table partners: "Who are your heroes?" After students discuss the question with their partners, Tanya charts her students' responses on the board under six columns: TV, Movies, Books, History, Sports, and People You Know. After charting the responses, Tanya asks her students, "Do heroes have to be famous?" She continues the lesson by introducing some heroes from the community as well as historical figures. She ends the lesson with a slideshow including a picture of Rosa Parks.

In later lessons, Tanya delves deeper into the notion of heroes by having students read articles and books on famous leaders during the Civil Rights Movement such as Rosa Parks and Ruby Bridges. Students also explore famous protests and boycotts such as the Montgomery bus boycott, grape boycott, 1960s lunch-counter sit-ins, May 1st marches, Justice for Janitors union picket line, and student budget cut march and walk-out. The unit ends with students discussing what they have learned and how they can work to make change within their communities.

Tanya used questioning as a means to elicit students' prior learning and to connect new learning to what students could already relate to. Her discussion on heroes was a way to inspire wonder in her students, for them to think about who they may perceive as a hero, what role heroes play in their lives, and what people do in their schools and communities to be perceived as heroes. In this case, Tanya wanted her students to learn about Rosa Parks and other protestors' roles in civil rights history. She hoped that her students would connect to these models of activism and think about how they can also "do heroic acts in their lives and connect this to social justice in their communities and world."

If Tanya was limited to her textbook, she could look for pictures of "heroes" in the curriculum. She could ask her students to think about questions such as:

- How does the textbook define a hero?
- Who is considered to be a hero?
- Who is not?
- What gender do you think of when you think of the word *hero*? Does this mean women cannot be heroes?
- Who are your heroes?

After this discussion, Tanya could integrate social studies content into language arts if she was limited with time. During her language arts period, she could continue the discussion about heroes by doing an interactive read-aloud with her students. The book could be about someone often recognized such as Cesar Chavez or Nelson Mandela or a story about someone less known, such as Ruby Bridges. The book *Through My Eyes* by Ruby Bridges (1999) is an autobiographical story of a 6-year-old girl who became the first Black student at the all-White William Frantz Public School in New Orleans, Louisiana, on November 14, 1960. In this way, students have multiple opportunities to gain deep understandings of what it means to be a hero, while the teacher meets social studies and language arts objectives.

For example, by using *Through My Eyes* as an interactive read-aloud with her students, Tanya could meet the following ELA Common Core Standards for Reading: Literature, grade 3:

Connecting to Common Core State Standards

Key Ideas and Details

RL.3.1. Ask and answer questions to demonstrate understanding of a text, referring explicitly to the text as the basis for the answers.

RL.3.3. Describe characters in a story (e.g., their traits, motivations, or feelings) and explain how their actions contribute to the sequence of events.

Tanya could explicitly teach each standard through minilessons during her language arts period, or during and after the read-aloud she could ask her students critical comprehension questions that address the third-grade Common Core Standards for reading such as:

- Who was the main character in the story? What characteristics would you choose to describe Ruby Bridges?
- What did Ruby Bridges do that impacted the future for others? How did she make change?
- How might you relate to Ruby Bridges? How do you struggle? What can you do to make change for others?

By teaching social studies and language arts as complementary subjects, Tanya can teach social studies from a critical perspective and address the essential elements of literacy.

Grace's Classroom—The Meaning of Community

In a second-grade classroom in New York City, Grace uses questioning as a means to present new information in a way students can understand. The objective of her lesson is for students to understand what a community is, how it works, and how they benefit from being part of a community.

To begin her lesson Grace asks her students these questions: "Who are the people in your community you see every day? Who are the people you don't see every day but who play a valuable role in your everyday lives? Who helps you who you may not notice?" She then shares the story of Lucy, a character in the book *A Street Called Home* (Robinson, 1997). Told from the girl's perspective, this book illustrates the characters that live and work in a middle-class Cleveland neighborhood.

Grace helps her students articulate and reflect upon what a community is, how it works, and how they benefit from being part of a community. By engaging students in a discussion about communities in relation to students' experiences with people in their own community, Grace builds a bridge between prior learning and new knowledge. After developing students' understanding of community, Grace reads the book to students then continues the lesson by having students write a story about a member of their community who has helped them.

Here, Grace connects social studies content and language arts. She asks students to build on their ideas of what a community is and who the members of their community might be. She elicits questions that ask students to share their prior learning and then reads to students a book that will deepen their understandings of a community. She chooses a book that is developmentally appropriate to her students.

By using a read-aloud to connect social studies content and language arts and providing a space to ask students critical comprehension questions about the text, Grace can cover the following ELA Common Core Standards for Reading, grade 2:

Connecting to Common Core State Standards
Key Ideas and Details
RL.2.1. Ask and answer such questions as who, what, where, when, why, and how to demonstrate understanding of key details in a text.
RL.2.3. Describe how characters in a story respond to major events and challenges.

By asking students critical questions about a text, including questions about the characters and details in the text, Grace can meet language arts Common Core Standards for reading. If Grace were required by her administration to teach from her textbook, she could juxtapose the read-aloud, *A Street Called Home* (Robinson, 1997), against the students' social studies textbook. While students read the passage on communities from their textbooks, Grace could ask her students to critically question the idea of community presented in their textbooks:

- How is a community represented in the textbook?
- Does this look like my community?
- Do the people in the community look like people in my community?
- What jobs do people have?
- What jobs do people have in my community?
- What is similar and what is different?

As Grace may be using the textbook as she is expected to do, she is also finding ways to make the curriculum critical by asking her students to question how the idea of community may be presented in their textbooks. She is also integrating language arts and social studies and meeting Common Core language arts standards by providing students with a space to ask and answer questions about the text and share their ideas and beliefs.

Tanya and Grace show how questioning can be used to connect new learning to students' experiences, interests, and background knowledge. By giving students the opportunity to build new learning from what they already know, children may be better able to grasp new information. Tanya and Grace also showed us how we can teach social justice–oriented lessons, integrate literacy, and meet language arts Common Core Standards.

To inspire wonder, we must carefully extend bridges between prior knowledge and students' learning, awakening and inviting students' questions. Teachers must pull from students what they already know and what they are interested in to provide a basis for students to understand, learn, and remember new concepts and ideas.

CONCLUSION

Wonder is an essential component to social justice teaching. When children are curious and inquisitive about subject matter, it opens the door for critical thinking and exploration. In this capacity, learning is presented to students as connected to their lives, interests, and beliefs, where voice is recognized and welcomed. Right from the start, students are challenged to critically think about the material presented to them, leading them to wonder about questions such as, "Why are there no people of color in the picture? Who was that document written for? Why was that person treated that way?" or "How can I also help my community? What emotions do I feel after learning about the event? Do I feel emotions such as sad, angry, proud, happy, upset?"

Strategies are presented in this chapter to help us think about ways in which we might introduce social justice–orientated social studies material to students and meet language arts Common Core Standards. We can use simulations and personal stories to evoke emotion in our students or an artifact analysis or questions to challenge students to question and think. Either way, our goal in inspiring wonder is to get students critically thinking about the subject matter.

Once a teacher has familiarized herself with the strategies presented in this chapter, the challenge becomes how to integrate the strategies into classroom practice, how to use pieces of the mandated curriculum and still approach social studies teaching from a critical perspective. We will return to this issue in each chapter of this book.

In this chapter, some of the strategies lend more to using direct pieces of a mandated curriculum, while others require more creativity. For example, an artifact analysis might introduce a fourth-grade unit on the California Missions. In textbooks California history is often portrayed as beginning with the Franciscan missionaries. What is excluded from the text is a view of Spanish settlement in California from a critical perspective, confronting the brutality of the missionaries against the Native Americans to look at slavery in the missions and Native American resistance to Californian Catholic missionaries. What we can take from textbooks is the pictures and documents often integrated into textbooks. This strategy encourages students to look at a historical event from a critical perspective, laying the groundwork for subsequent lessons which will delve deeper into the subject matter. Textbooks can provide a background for teaching and also offer opportunities for critical analysis of history.

Guiding simulations may require more time, but they can be a powerful way of increasing students' awareness, disrupting misconceptions, and building empathy. We can find ideas on the Internet, in examples provided in this book, or from other critical resources. Personal stories may be collected through guest speakers in the community or an online search. Publications by Rethinking Schools have poems and stories from voices often underrepresented in our textbooks that can encourage and inspire wonder, curiosity, and intrigue in our students. If limited with time, you could integrate stories into a language arts period through shared reading or interactive read-alouds.

Teaching for social justice requires us to not only be committed to ideals that promote fairness, moral responsibility, and social action, but also require us to know how to navigate a context of mandated curriculum and accountability. There will be times when a teacher will be able to draw from standard teaching resources (e.g., textbooks) and there will be times to negotiate curricular constraints to teach what one wants to teach. As teachers, we must validate students' curiosity, wonder, and intrigue and find ways to encourage our students to be critical thinkers. Teaching social studies for social justice is teaching our students to effectively critique and change the world.

REFLECTION EXERCISES

Below are reflection exercises to help extend these concepts into classroom practice:

1. Think of a student in your classroom. Jot down everything you know about him or her. You can use a graphic organizer, like a web, to help you. Based on what you know about this student, what are ways you can connect content to the student's interests, background, and experiences?
2. Consider the next lessons in social studies you are planning to teach. If you don't have time to teach social studies, think about language arts. What are ways you can integrate social justice issues into the lessons? What strategies might you use from the ones discussed in this chapter?
3. When developing a social justice–oriented social studies lesson or unit, how might you begin the lesson by inspiring wonder in your students? How will you elicit prior learning? What strategies will you draw from? What resources will you use?
4. If you are limited to using mandated curriculum, such as textbooks, in the classroom, what are some documents you could pull from the textbook? How might these documents inspire wonder and critical thinking in your students?
5. What scaffolds or support systems would you use to support your English language learners and special needs students in the teacher practice examples shared above?

CHAPTER 3

Painting the Picture

AFTER WE HAVE worked to inspire wonder in our students by awakening their curiosity, the next step will be to paint a picture of the historical event from multiple perspectives, including the perspective of people and groups who often remain silenced in our textbooks. The purpose of doing this is to dispel students' misconceptions, challenge students to be critical thinkers, allow students to create their own judgments about history, and instill a sense of injustice in students. In this chapter we learn how to uncover the past by challenging students' misconceptions around historical events and getting them thinking deeply and critically about social studies content through the exploration of multiple perspectives.

Social studies content, as portrayed in our textbooks, is often a composition of historical accounts that leave out the voices of those deeply involved in the event. Let's take for example the Mexican-American War. In a short paragraph a textbook may briefly describe America's success in controlling a half million square miles of Mexican territory. The textbook may explain how Americans were driven by the idea of Manifest Destiny and their desire to expand across the North American continent. Under Manifest Destiny, Americans believed that they had the God-given right to expand the country's borders from "sea to shining sea," whether or not the land was owned and lived on by others.

Missing from the story is the complexity behind the event and how people's actions, individually and collectively, influenced our society and the distribution of power and resources. When the border moved after the Mexican-American War, Mexicans inside the United States were supposed to be guaranteed by the United States the same rights as citizens. However, political restrictions were used to "disenfranchise Mexicans" and lessen "the ability of Mexicans to claim their rights as citizens" (Takaki, 2008, p. 167). This action by the United States forced many rancheros to sell their land for minimal fees, leaving once-wealthy Mexican land owners to work in the field.

The mainstream narrative perpetuated in our textbooks denies the voices and histories of many members of our society (Sleeter, 2011). Textbooks often portray history as a string of oversimplified facts that deny students opportunities to think deeply about the past and understand how racism and discrimination worked to give power and resources to some and deny power and resources to others (Loewen, 2007). In our textbooks history is told most commonly from the perspective of Whites, predominately White European males, in often oversimplified stories, "more accurately categorized as historical myths" (Levstik & Barton, 2005, p. 8). As Sleeter (2011) notes, "Whites continue to receive the most attention and appear in the widest variety of roles, dominating story lines and lists of accomplishments" (p. 2). The limited narrative or partial story presented in textbooks denies students the opportunity to see their ancestors as contributory and important members of society. Levstik and Barton (2005) explain that "students who do not see themselves as members of groups who had agency in the past or power in the present, who are invisible in history, lack viable models for the future" (p. 3). In this sense, students may see themselves and members of their group as silent on public issues, invisible and unimportant to society, and compliant to the oppression they face. Such representations of history offer children inauthentic portrayals of history that are not inclusive of the contributory actions of members of our society outside of the dominant narrative.

Because textbooks most often illuminate a Eurocentric perspective, one that highlights the perspective of European males, students' access to information surrounding the past may be limited to historical assertions that may not always be true. For example, Loewen (2007) examined the portrayal of Christopher Columbus in history textbooks. He found almost everything in the accounts to be "either wrong or unverifiable" (p. 32) such as underplaying the accomplishments and contributions of previous explorers, glorifying the role of Columbus and his "discovery," and minimizing Columbus's horrific treatment of the native Taino people. The historical myth of Columbus perpetuated in many textbooks prevents students from having the opportunity to critically examine the past, understand history from the Taino perspective, and see the contributions of so many others who made the voyage prior to Columbus.

This chapter discusses how you can paint a true historical picture for students and work to challenge students' misconceptions and uncover historical events from the examination of multiple perspectives. Included are strategies to paint the picture with examples of teacher practice, ways to connect social studies content to language arts, meet language arts Common Core Standards, and draw on mandated curricular materials to find space to integrate the strategies discussed in this chapter.

EXPLORING MULTIPLE PERSPECTIVES

Students need opportunities to question how and why they know what they know. They need to be able to examine their misconceptions around history including historical myths of Christopher Columbus "discovering" America. Additionally, students need to know that historical accounts are selective and are based on an interpretation that is determined by someone who decides how to tell a story. As Levstik and Barton (2005) explain, "whenever history is told as a narrative, someone has to decide when the story begins and ends, what is included or left out, and which events appear as problems or solutions" (p. 6). Thus history involves a retelling from a certain group or person's interpretation. However, as storytellers determine what to include and not include, we may miss out on the perspectives of other people and groups deeply involved in the historical event. We need to help our students recognize that this is the way history is written and show them how to find additional stories.

As we paint the picture, we can offer a historical narrative that is inclusive of the voices and perspectives that are often glossed over or minimized in our current textbooks. When studying history, we must see, hear, and feel the contributions, resistance, and actions of all of those who have contributed to our society and world. We may feel empowered and motivated to make change in our own communities as we learn how our ancestors fought for their freedoms and resisted oppression and discrimination. We may also feel empowered to learn how we can serve as allies, just as other members of our society did, to help others in their fight for rights and freedom. In this way, we can grapple with history, understand historical events from multiple perspectives, and learn from the struggles of others. We can become "history detectives" seeking to get as close to truth as possible, believing that no single person, even those who witnessed the event, can know the entire story (Cowhey, 2006).

By teaching multiple perspectives, we can help students realize that there is more than one story that can be told about any event that happens (Wade, 2007). For example, we can study the Civil Rights Movement through the eyes of the thousands of individuals who "performed the many, complicated acts of resistance that aimed to change the course of history" (Menkart, Murray, & View, 2004, p. 410), such as Ruby Bridges. We can think about Christopher Columbus's arrival from the perspective of the Tainos, and we can examine the Chinese Exclusion Act from the perspective of the Chinese. By delving deep into history, through the perspective of those outside of the White narrative, we may begin to construct a vision of history that elucidates the struggles of all people for justice, purporting pluralism, rather than ranking one group against the other. In other words, by honoring and exploring multiple perspectives, we are seeing the achievement, struggles, and acts of resistance as important and integral to the collective creation of our society, country, and world.

When painting the picture, our goal is to "help students uncover the past rather than cover it" (Loewen, 2010, p. 19). For this reason, students are critically involved with the texts they are presented with. As all our stories are only partially known (Levstik & Barton, 2005), students are expected to think

TABLE 3.1. Essential Comprehension Strategies

Using background knowledge	Students use prior knowledge to understand text and information given to them.
Inferring	Students make predictions and draw conclusions based on the evidence given to them.
Determining importance	Students establish the main points in the text or argument.
Synthesizing	Students piece together numerous details to construct a single understanding
Questioning	Students ask critical questions as a means to clarify or dispute what they are reading.
Creating mental images	Students visualize what they are reading or imagine people, places, and events in history.
Making connections	Students make connections to what they are reading: • Text-to-self connections made between the reader's personal experiences and the text • Text-to-text connections made between a text being read and a text previously read • Text-to-world connections made between the text being read and events occurring in the world.

critically about the historical assertions presented to them (Loewen, 2010). Students work to uncover the past and critically examine various sources of information from multiple perspectives to see the way history changes and moves as more information, evidence, and understandings are collected.

BUILDING STUDENTS' CRITICAL THINKING SKILLS AND READING COMPREHENSION

In thinking of ways to integrate literacy with social studies, one aspect of literacy that is intrinsically linked to critical thinking is developing students' reading comprehension. When teaching students to read, we give students explicit instruction in decoding, fluency, word analysis, text structures, and vocabulary, and also teach students to think critically and make judgments about what they read. Reading comprehension strategies are commonly taught in a comprehensive literacy program (described in Chapter 1) often through guided reading, independent reading, read-alouds, or shared reading. Comprehension strategies teach students to be metacognitive—to be able to think about thinking—so that they can "read with deeper, longer-lasting understanding" (Keene & Zimmerman, 2007, p. 33). Some essential comprehension strategies are included in Table 3.1.

Many of the comprehension strategies in Table 3.1 are the same strategies we use in social studies to encourage our students to be critical thinkers. In social studies, like language arts, we are teaching students to be metacognitive. Students are commonly asked to *infer, synthesize,* and/or *question* texts such as newspapers, textbooks, picture books, or websites. Students may also use strategies taught through reading comprehension, such as *making connections* and *creating visual images,* when asked to examine primary or secondary resources or engage in a simulation that looks at a historical event from multiple perspectives.

For example, in a document analysis students are expected to *infer* and critically *question* a primary source document they receive. Students may ask themselves questions such as: Who benefits from the document? Who does not benefit from the document? Why was the document created? Students may also use their *background knowledge* to help them make assertions about the document. A student could also lean on *mental images* to imagine what life was like for people when the document was written. Comprehension strategies taught during a language arts block are both necessary for learning to read deeply and to think critically across all subject areas, especially social studies.

Because the reading comprehension strategies listed in Table 3.1 are so commonly used in social justice–oriented social studies teaching, it may not be difficult to link social studies teaching with language arts. For example, when we teach social studies content we are encouraging our students to be critical thinkers. When we engage students in comprehension strategy instruction, we are preparing them "to be active, critical, and strategic readers" (Keene & Zimmerman, 2007, p. 27). If we begin to see comprehension strategies as linked to social justice–oriented social studies teaching, we may be better able to draw connections between language arts and social studies content. We will return to these strategies throughout the book, especially in this chapter, as these comprehension strategies are an essential component to challenging our students to be critical thinkers.

As we explicitly teach reading comprehension strategies through social studies content, we can potentially meet the Common Core Anchor Standards for Reading that follow on the next page.

Each of the language arts Common Core Anchor Standards listed in the box can be covered in social studies lessons if the teacher explicitly draws attention to the specific standard being addressed. For example, teachers could ask their students to analyze and critically question a text to determine whose point of view is shared and whose point of view is silenced. Through this activity, a teacher could explicitly teach students the reading comprehension strategy of "questioning" and also meet language arts Common Core Anchor Standards because while questioning, students are learning to delineate and evaluate arguments and specific claims in text. Students are also learning to comprehend complex literary texts independently and proficiently.

Connecting to Common Core State Standards

Key Ideas and Details

Read closely to determine what the text says explicitly and to make logical inferences from it; cite specific textual evidence when writing or speaking to support conclusions drawn from the text.
Determine central ideas or themes of a text and analyze their development; summarize the key supporting details and ideas.
Analyze how and why individuals, events, and ideas develop and interact over the course of a text.

Craft and Structure

Interpret words and phrases as they are used in a text, including determining technical, connotative, and figurative meanings, and analyze how specific word choices shape meaning or tone.

Integration of Knowledge and Ideas

Integrate and evaluate content presented in diverse media and formats, including visually and quantitatively, as well as in words.
Delineate and evaluate the argument and specific claims in a text, including the validity of the reasoning as well as the relevance and sufficiency of the evidence.
Analyze how two or more texts address similar themes or topics in order to build knowledge or to compare the approaches the authors take.

Range of Reading and Level of Text Complexity

Read and comprehend complex literary and informational texts independently and proficiently.

By building bridges between language arts and social studies, we can meet language arts Common Core Standards, find greater space to teach social studies, and guide our students through a learning process where subject areas are taught jointly, instead of in isolation.

USING CHILDREN'S LITERATURE

It's not uncommon for students to despise social studies. If and when social studies is taught, instruction often consists of reading from a textbook and then answering a set of questions. Loewen (2007) affirms the fact that textbooks can be uninteresting. He shares, "The stories that history textbooks tell are predictable; every problem has already been solved or is about to be solved. Textbooks exclude conflict or real suspense" (p. 5). Moreover, textbooks "leave out most of what we need to know about the American past" (p. 7), which includes portraying the perspectives of those often left out of the mainstream narrative. If we narrow social studies teaching to textbooks, students most likely will be given a sanitized version of history that may work to perpetuate patriotism and compliancy and do little to forward pluralism and solidarity.

Read-alouds

By integrating children's literature into your social studies teaching, you may also be able to incorporate many of the reading comprehension strategies we listed in the previous section into your teaching. For example, Parvati, a third-grade teacher in New York City read aloud *Harvesting Hope: The Story of Cesar Chavez* (Krull, 2003) to her students during her language arts period to paint the picture for her students of the Farmworkers Movement in 1956. The book details the life of Cesar Chavez and his efforts to protest the working conditions of the farmworkers in California. In the book there is a picture of Cesar Chavez as a child wearing a sign that says, "I am a clown. I speak Spanish." During the read-aloud, Parvati stopped at this picture to model the strategy of "making connections" for her students. She shared:

> When I look at this picture I remember my own feelings as a child in elementary school. I remember feeling like I had to change my name to Patricia so that I could fit in with the rest of my classmates. I wanted to be called Parvati, but I knew no one could properly pronounce my name. Instead of teaching them the correct pronunciation, I felt more comfortable changing my name. This is a text-to-self connection. I am connecting an experience of mine to something that happened to Cesar Chavez in the book. Let's see if you can make some connections.

After Parvati shared her own experience, she asked her predominately first- and second-generation Latino students to share some of their thoughts. She asked, "What do you think of this picture? How do you think Cesar felt when wearing the sign? Can you connect to what Cesar may be feeling? Does the discrimination Cesar is facing remind you of someone else you know or a character in a book you've read?" Through this discussion, Parvati elicits many important aspects of teaching: (1) She chooses a book that is culturally relevant. Many of her students are Latino and also have parents and family who work in the fields and for this reason students may be more likely to connect to the story. (2) She models for her students how to make connections. (3) She develops student reading comprehension by asking them to make connections. (4) She uses a read-aloud, in a narrative format, to paint the picture and teach students about history.

By integrating language arts and social studies and explicitly teaching the reading comprehension strategy of making connections, Parvati can cover the following ELA Common Core Standards for Reading: Literature, grade 3:

Connecting to Common Core State Standards

Key Ideas and Details:

RL.3.1. Ask and answer questions to demonstrate understanding of a text, referring explicitly to the text as the basis for the answers.

RL.3.2. Recount stories, including fables, folktales, and myths from diverse cultures; determine the central message, lesson, or moral and explain how it is conveyed through key details in the text.

RL.3.3. Describe characters in a story (e.g., their traits, motivations, or feelings) and explain how their actions contribute to the sequence of events.

Through her lesson, Paravati is asking questions that challenge students to demonstrate their understanding of the text, recount and summarize key details, and describe how characters contributed to the story. The read-aloud activity allows Parvati the opportunity to get her students thinking critically about the Farmworkers Movement, build students' reading comprehension, and meet language arts Common Core Standards.

Read-alouds can be an important way of sharing social studies content and perspectives that are not visible in our textbooks. Often, teachers only consider fiction books for read-alouds; nonfiction books can be great read-alouds as well, especially if you can find them in a big book format. The focus of the read-aloud is to enhance "students' comprehension by engaging them in the reading process before, during, and after reading" (Tompkins, 2010, p. 439). First, teachers introduce the book, build students' background knowledge, and preview important vocabulary before beginning to read. Second, the teacher engages students during the reading by asking them comprehension questions, modeling comprehension strategies like making connections, and reinforcing key vocabulary. Last, the teacher reflects with students on the book and discusses key ideas that emerged from the book. For example:

- What was the author's message or intent?
- How do you feel about the main character in the book? Can you relate to him or her in any way?
- Who was the book written for?

- Whose perspective do we get to hear?
- Whose perspective do we not get to hear?
- Who may have been missing from the story line?

By asking questions like these, a teacher is not only checking students' understanding of the text, she is also challenging her students to think critically about the text and be aware of the voices who dominate the story line. If you are limited by the amount of time you have to teach social studies or have to teach from the textbook during your social studies period, you can enact the read-aloud during your language arts period. If you do plan to teach from your textbook during your social studies period, be sure to make concrete connections for your students between the read-aloud and textbooks. For example, a simple way to do this is to ask, "What did you learn during the read-aloud about _____ that was not in the textbook? Why do you think this perspective or story was missing from the textbook?"

Book Reviews

In a book review, groups of approximately four students are given one children's picture book and they must do three things with it: (1) read the book, (2) assess the book for bias, and (3) learn from the historical account presented in the book. For example, when teaching students about Christopher Columbus the following strategy can help paint the picture of what really happened during the Columbus and Taino encounter. Each group is given a picture book about Christopher Columbus. Some books lean more toward a Eurocentric perspective, while others toward the Taino perspective. In groups, students read the book and then critique the book's treatment of Columbus and the Tainos. Students answer the following questions on their handouts:

- How factually accurate was the account?
- What was omitted or left out from the text that in your judgment would be important for a full understanding of Columbus?
- What motives does this book give to Columbus? Compare those with his real motives.
- Who does this book get you to root for and how is that accomplished? (Are the authors horrified at the treatment of Indians or thrilled that Columbus makes it to the New World?)
- How do the publishers use illustrations? What do these communicate about Columbus and his "enterprise"?

After students have had a substantial amount of time to critically analyze the book and write down their answers to the questions, one volunteer from each group comes forward and charts their group's answers on a large piece of chart paper (see Table 3.2).

TABLE 3.2. Whole-Class Chart of Answers for Students to Compare

Name of Book	Factually Accurate	Omitted	Motive	Who Do You Root For?	Illustrations
Encounter (Yolen, 1996)					

When all groups have finished charting their answers, the whole class comes together to discuss the findings from the book reviews using the following questions:

- In your opinion, why does each book portray the Columbus/Taino encounter the way it does?
- What themes were prevalent across all of the books?
- Can you think of any groups in our society who might have an interest in people having an inaccurate view of history?
    - ✓ Who benefits from the historical account (the way it is presented)?
    - ✓ What do you think about changing the holiday "Columbus Day" to "Indigenous Day?"

Through the book review, students begin to see the bias prevalent in all texts, including children's literature. They see themes across the books that portray Columbus as kind, holy, intelligent, and noble. Few children's books illustrate the horrific treatment of the Tainos or Columbus's greed for gold and power.

The book review strategy allows students to delve deeply into social studies content through a critical analysis, see a perspective that may be silenced or limited in social studies textbooks, and learn about people, communities, and history through a more interesting and engaging medium than their textbooks. Because students are grouped, collaborative learning also creates a safe space for all students to share ideas and learn from each other.

The book review strategy could be taught during a language arts period as the strategy lends itself to meeting many Common Core Anchor Standards for Reading such as the ones seen on page 48.

When we embed reading comprehension strategies such as questioning and synthesizing into a social justice–oriented social studies curriculum, we are working intentionally to teach social studies and literacy as complementary subjects. In this way, we can meet language arts Common Core Standards and find space to teach social studies for social justice.

Connecting to Common Core State Standards

Key Ideas and Details

Read closely to determine what the text says explicitly and to make logical inferences from it; cite specific textual evidence when writing or speaking to support conclusions drawn from the text.

Determine central ideas or themes of a text and analyze their development; summarize the key supporting details and ideas.

Analyze how and why individuals, events, and ideas develop and interact over the course of a text.

Craft and Structure

Interpret words and phrases as they are used in a text, including determining technical, connotative, and figurative meanings, and analyze how specific word choices shape meaning or tone.

Analyze the structure of texts, including how specific sentences, paragraphs, and larger portions of the text (e.g., a section, chapter, scene, or stanza) relate to each other and the whole.

Assess how point of view or purpose shapes the content and style of a text.

Integration of Knowledge and Ideas

Integrate and evaluate content presented in diverse media and formats, including visually and quantitatively, as well as in words.

Delineate and evaluate the argument and specific claims in a text, including the validity of the reasoning as well as the relevance and sufficiency of the evidence.

Analyze how two or more texts address similar themes or topics in order to build knowledge or to compare the approaches the authors take.

Range of Reading and Level of Text Complexity

Read and comprehend complex literary and informational texts independently and proficiently.

Literature Circles

Like the previous strategies, literature circles can help deepen students' understanding of social studies content through texts other than mandated curriculum. As Tompkins (2010) notes, "one of the best ways to nurture students' love of reading and ensure that they become lifelong readers is through literature circles—small, student-led book discussion groups" (p. 336). In literature circles students come together in flexible groups formed by book

TABLE 3.3. Literature Circle Roles

Word wizard	Find words that the group may not understand, look for meaning in a dictionary
Illustrator	Draw a scene from the assigned reading
Discussion director	Prepare discussion questions for the group
Summarizer	Summarize reading
Connector	Make connections between texts, world, and self

choice that meet on a regular schedule to read and discuss readings. Students are assigned specified roles (e.g., word wizard, summarizer) and use notes to guide both their reading and discussion. The discussion is generated by students. The teacher's role is that of a facilitator.

On the first day of literature circles, present students approximately six books and give them a description of each book including the length of the text and the difficulty of the words. After describing the books, ask them to choose three books and rank them in order of preference. Based on their rankings, group students according to which book they are interested in and which book is most accessible to them given their reading level. The next day in their literature circle groups, students determine how many pages they will read for each session. Each literature circle is expected to read one day and then meet the next. They follow this pattern until they finish the book. They are then required to create a project to showcase their book (e.g., game board, skit, alternate ending to book). Some of the literature circle roles I used in my class are shown in Table 3.3.

Students alternate among the roles in their groups. While reading silently, students fill out a worksheet to guide them through their task. For example, if a student was the discussion director for the group that day, the worksheet would have a description of the role and some sample questions to help the students. The roles were also described and modeled by me at the beginning of the year.

When focused on exploring social studies content, literature circles can offer students the opportunity to work collaboratively to uncover the past. During literature circle meetings, students get to meet with their groups to critically discuss the perspectives and bias prevalent in their book. They can also juxtapose their literature circle reading with what they read in their textbooks. It is in this way that students begin to paint a picture for themselves of what really happened in the past. Through literature circles, you can teach social studies content and meet Common Core Anchor Standards for Speaking and Listening:

> ### Connecting to Common Core State Standards
>
> *Comprehension and Collaboration*
>
> Prepare for and participate effectively in a range of conversations and collaborations with diverse partners, building on others' ideas and expressing their own clearly and persuasively.

Students may find it easier to relate to characters in a historical fiction book than to the stories presented in their textbooks. When students are able to connect with historical figures, they may be better able to empathize with different perspectives and identify with those who may have shared a similar struggle. Children's literature is a great supplement to a social studies textbook, as students may find the reading more interesting and accessible than their textbooks. By using children's literature, teachers can paint a picture for students of history that is more inclusive of others' perspectives and points of view.

Tanisha's Classroom—Ruby Bridges

Tanisha is a fifth-grade teacher in a New York City public school that is wholly Black and Latino. She uses the book, *Through My Eyes* (Bridges, 1999), a story about Ruby Bridges, to paint the picture of the injustices people of color faced during the Civil Rights Movement.

To begin, Tanisha asks students to think about differences they can observe among themselves and their classmates (e.g., eye color, hair, skin color). After students have had a few minutes to think, Tanisha asks her students to share their observations as a whole group so that she can chart them on the board. Tanisha reminds her students that there are many differences among their classmates and that each difference makes them unique and special.

Tanisha then asks students to think about a hypothetical situation: What if some class members were given certain privileges and other class members were not? What if some class members could participate in activities and others could not because they were different? For example, what if only girls could eat their lunch inside and boys had to eat their lunch outside even if it was raining or snowing? Or children who were left-handed had to attend a different school than right-handed children? Tanisha then asks her students, "What if you couldn't do everything other children got to do just because you were different in some way?" After sharing these questions with the class, Tanisha opens up the discussion to the whole group.

When the discussion comes to an end, Tanisha introduces the book *Through My Eyes* (Bridges, 1999). She explains that Ruby Bridges is someone who was viewed by others as being different. During the Civil Rights Movement, Black students had to be tested to go to White schools. Ruby was one of the few Black children to pass the test and be able to attend a White school.

After students share their ideas, Tanisha continues reading and pauses frequently to have students turn and talk to each other, a strategy that helps build reading comprehension. Following the read-aloud, Tanisha asks her students to reflect in their notebooks on Ruby Bridges's decision to attend an all White school. She says, "On one hand, her father felt nervous because angry segregationists would hurt her family. On the other hand, Ruby can go to a better school. How would you feel if this were your child? You saw some of the pictures in the book—everything is segregated. How would you feel putting your child in an integrated school? The father brought up good points and the mother brought up good points. Put yourself in their shoes. What would you do?" After a few minutes, she asks the students to turn and talk to their partners about what they wrote.

Tanisha ends the lesson by having students work in small groups. Each of the groups is responsible for answering the following set of questions:

- How did Ruby demonstrate courage?
- If you were Ruby, what would you have done? Would you have done anything differently? Why or why not?
- Were all White people bad? Did they all hate Black people? What information in the story leads you to believe this?
- In what ways have Ruby's actions affected your lives?

After the students are finished, they present their answers to the rest of the group.

The activity provides an important platform for Tanisha to transition into the story of Ruby Bridges and study the discrimination Ruby faced. She wants her students to know how the contributions of people in the past greatly influence and affect how we live today.

By using the read-aloud *Through My Eyes* to paint the picture and drawing attention to the reading comprehension strategy of making connections, Tanisha could potentially meet the following ELA Common Core Standards for Reading: Literature and Speaking and Listening, grade 5:

Connecting to Common Core State Standards

Comprehension and Collaboration

SL.5.1. Engage effectively in a range of collaborative discussions (one-on-one, in groups, and teacher-led) with diverse partners on grade 5 topics and texts, building on others' ideas and expressing their own clearly.

This lesson could easily be taught in a language arts period. As read-alouds are an important piece of a comprehensive literacy program, Tanisha has the opportunity to teach language arts and social studies in an integrated manner.

To make the integration concrete to students, Tanisha could preface the read-aloud by saying, "Today we will be learning about an important event in our country's history. We will be learning about the event through the eyes of a 6-year-old girl from Mississippi. While you are learning about her courage and actions, I will be discussing an important reading comprehension strategy: making connections. Throughout the read-aloud, I will stop the discussion to ask you to make connections." After this introduction, Tanisha could then do a minilesson on the different types of connections: text-to-self, text-to-text, and text-to-world. Tanisha could model each of these connections for her students. As Tanisha reads the book to her students, she could model how to make connections by thinking aloud.

If Tanisha were required to follow a mandated curriculum, read-alouds could be used as a supplementary text. For example, after the teacher previewed important vocabulary and concepts, students could read (either through independent reading or a shared reading) sections of the textbook to build their background. Then stories such as the one of Ruby Bridges could be read after the textbook reading and juxtaposed against what was presented in their textbook. The teacher could ask questions such as:

- Why do you think the story of Ruby Bridges is not in the textbook?
- Do you think her story is important? Why?
- Who do you think contributed to the Civil Rights Movement?
- How and why did they contribute?
- Would you do the same?
- How do their contributions impact you today?

Critical thinking questions, such as the ones listed above, allow students to see the bias in texts and seek alternatives to the mainstream dominant text. Students can also see how children their age can be contributory and important members of society and can also work to make change in their society.

Because of the focus on language arts and math at Tanisha's school, this social studies lesson was an isolated lesson for her. She did not have the opportunity to expand on the lesson. If she had time, she might be able to continue with the framework presented in this book. For example, she could have extended the students' understanding through a series of learning opportunities including:

- A documentary on the Civil Rights Movement that includes the perspective of women who battled for their rights, such as the right to vote (painting the picture)
- Literature circles to discuss the documentary
- Biographies of different civil rights activists (painting the picture),

with student groups creating a PowerPoint presentation on the book they read

- A discussion of the parallel story that led up to the Supreme Court decision in *Brown v. Board of Education* that decided that segregation in "separate but equal" schools is inherently unequal and unconstitutional
- Whole-group discussion connecting the past and the present (connecting the past to the present)
- Research projects in which each group researches and studies a group that is fighting for freedom today and their efforts to resist discrimination and prejudice
- A whole-group project to find a space where they can make change just like Ruby Bridges made change in her community, such as a petition for healthier lunches, writing letters to their congresspeople to save art and music at their school, or raising money to supply fresh drinking water to children in India (facilitating change)

In any case, finding opportunities, just as Tanisha did, to teach a social justice–oriented social studies lesson when limited to reading and math is an important first step. For many teachers, finding ways to integrate social studies content into language arts is the only way they might be able to find time to teach social studies. Teachers can use children's literature against textbook readings to ask questions like "Why do you think the textbook does not include the story of _____?" In this way, students may begin to see their textbooks as a partial story that is often condensed or simplified. Outside resources, such as children's literature, offer students social studies content that is inclusive of voices and perspectives that are often glossed over or minimized in textbooks.

Critical Thinking

As bias is prevalent in all books, it is important for teachers to take the time to critically analyze texts with their students. While teachers ask comprehension questions, they can also ask critical reading questions such as the following:

- Who was this text written for?
- Who benefits from this text?
- Who does not benefit from the text?
- How is this story different from the historical account presented in your textbooks?
- Why do you think the stories are different?

In preparing our students to be critical thinkers, we must paint a picture of history to our students that embraces plurality. By providing students with children's literature as a secondary resource to textbooks, students are given the opportunity to grapple with multiple texts that elicit multiple perspectives. They can examine texts for bias and find intersections and contradictions between texts to formulate what they think really happened in history. By hearing the perspectives of those often silenced in textbooks through children's literature and outside texts, students can gain empathy and a sense of injustice for groups who have been discriminated against and oppressed in our nation's history. Students can also learn from those who have fought for change, like Ruby Bridges, as inspiration to make change within their own communities.

When sharing multiple perspectives, we must be careful to not portray one perspective as right over another. If we do this, we take away our students' ability to grapple with history and find meaning and understanding on their own. We may also take away students' opportunity to see humanity in all people.

ROLE PLAY AND SIMULATIONS

In the previous chapter I discussed how teachers can use simulations to generate wonder and help students understand and relate to people and events from another time or place. In this chapter I show how a simulation can be used to deepen students' understandings around social studies content and challenge historical myths. According to Schmidt (2007), simulations offer students the opportunity to relive historical events from multiple perspectives and uncover the past for themselves:

> Simulations allow students to understand the nature of the event or have an experience similar to the people who went through it. In addition, they challenge students to exercise critical thinking. . . . Successful simulations encourage historic empathy by forcing students to approach situations from different points of view and grapple with their emotions. (p. 69)

From this assertion, we see how simulations can work to build students' critical thinking and allow students to struggle to piece together multiple stories of the past. Although we cannot physically enter into history, we can "know and feel enough historical details to sense how complex and multifaceted the story is" (Cowhey, 2006, p. 161). We, as teachers, can create opportunities for students to see and hear multiple perspectives and experience history through the eyes of others. Students then, may learn to empathize with groups of people whose histories they may have never known. Moreover, students may learn from others how to find courage and overcome adversity to make change within their schools, communities, and world.

Role plays work in a similar way. In a role play students may take on a certain character or persona during the simulation. Role play and simulation are especially important for the teaching and learning of social studies. As Singer and Singer (1992) assert, "the growth of intelligence is nurtured by make-believe play, as this is the primary means the child has for assimilating the reality of the world into existing experience" (p. 40). In other words, role play and simulations offer students the opportunity to merge the present with the past, to build deep understandings they may never receive from textbooks.

Role play and simulation can also work to make learning more accessible to English language learners. For many, content vocabulary, if not taught explicitly, may hinder these students from accessing important social studies content. Through role play and simulation, students are offered an alternative medium, besides their textbooks, for accessing social studies content. By engaging in the role play or simulation, students can feel and experience history. Role plays and simulations can serve as great tools for building background. Students may be better able to access dense textbook material after engaging in an imaginative entry into a historical event through an activity such as a role play or simulation.

In using simulations in the classroom to inspire wonder, teachers can meet the following Common Core Anchor Standards for Speaking and Listening:

Connecting to Common Core State Standards

Comprehension and Collaboration

Prepare for and participate effectively in a range of conversations and collaborations with diverse partners, building on others' ideas and expressing their own clearly and persuasively.

If we engage students in a discussion after a simulation, we can provide a space for students to think critically about their experiences surrounding the simulation. Through discussion, we can deepen students' understanding of critical historical content and meet language arts Common Core Standards that focus on teaching students to participate and share ideas.

Susan's Classroom—Chinese Exclusion Act

Susan is a fourth-grade teacher in San Francisco, California. She uses a simulation as an initial introduction to the treatment of the Chinese at Angel Island as a result of the Chinese Exclusion Act in 1882.

The room is set up with an interrogation section at the front of the room and a detainment section on the rug. To begin the lesson, Susan pretends that she is a government official in charge of interrogating students. As an official, she must decide if the students officially belong in the class. The students wait in a line outside of the classroom to be questioned. She explains to them, "So you students all say that you are part of Room 19? I'm not sure you are telling the truth. If you are, you will be able to answer my questions. If not, you will need to stay over there in detainment." Susan points to the rug.

Susan then puts stickers on several students randomly. These students are allowed to sit at their desks without questioning, and should take their seats and observe. Susan (in the role as interrogator) explains to her students in line that they will be asked a series of questions and they have to answer them accurately. Susan then asks each student several questions from the following list:

- What is your full name?
- How many windows are there in this classroom?
- What direction does the door face?
- Who sits at your table?
- What are their middle names?
- Who sits at the second table closest to the door?
- Who is the oldest student in the classroom?
- What is his/her favorite subject?
- How many pencils are in your desk?
- How far is your house from the school?
- What is your teacher's full name? Her middle name? How do you spell it?
- Where did your teacher grow up?

When a student cannot answer a question, the teacher says, "I'm sorry. I'm not sure you really are who you say you are. Please step over to the rug for detainment." If the teacher is satisfied with the responses, she gives the student a sticker and sends him to his desk to be "free."

After the simulation is finished, the class sits in a circle on the floor and Susan leads her students in a discussion about their feelings during the simulation. Susan asks her students:

- How did it feel to be questioned?
- What did you think of the questions? Were they easy or hard?
- Did you feel like it was fair or unfair?
- If you got a sticker at the beginning, how did you feel?
- How did you feel when you got accepted into the classroom?
- How did you feel when you got rejected from the classroom?
- How did you feel when you were waiting to be questioned?
- What was it like to watch other people get questioned?
- How does this relate to Angel Island?

After the discussion Susan uses part of her language arts period to read aloud from the book *Landed* (Lee & Choi, 2006). The book is about a 12-year-old boy, Sun, who wants to leave his village for America. After a long voyage to America, Sun is detained on Angel Island because of the 1882 Chinese Exclusion Act. Sun must take a detailed oral exam in English before he can go ashore.

Susan uses simulation to paint a picture of what really happened to the Chinese during the Chinese Exclusion Act. She maintains the role of a government official to show students what it was like for the Chinese once they were detained at Angel Island. Through the simulation, students can experience the grave discrimination the Chinese experienced and the unlawful actions that were taken to keep them off American soil. They can also learn key social studies content vocabulary in context, such as the word *detainment*. This is especially helpful for our English language learners.

Susan supports the simulation by building background with her students through a read-aloud. The read-aloud directly parallels what students are learning about the Chinese Exclusion Act and Angel Island. In this way, Susan is creating a clear connection between language arts and social studies. While reading the story of Sun to her students, Susan could use important reading comprehension strategies such as making inferences, questioning, or creating mental images. All of these strategies help deepen students' understanding of the text while simultaneously challenging students to think critically about this historical event. By using the read-aloud as a platform to build students' background knowledge and modeling and teaching reading comprehension strategies, Susan could meet the following ELA Common Core Standards for Reading: Literature, grade 4:

Connecting to Common Core State Standards

Key Ideas and Details

RL.4.1. Refer to details and examples in a text when explaining what the text says explicitly and when drawing inferences from the text.

RL.4.2. Determine a theme of a story, drama, or poem from details in the text; summarize the text.

RL.4.3. Describe in depth a character, setting, or event in a story or drama, drawing on specific details in the text (e.g., a character's thoughts, words, or actions).

Integration of Knowledge and Ideas

RL.4.9. Compare and contrast the treatment of similar themes and topics (e.g., opposition of good and evil) and patterns of events (e.g., the quest) in stories, myths, and traditional literature from different cultures.

By drawing attention to the Common Core Standards, Susan can use an activity such as a read-aloud to meet specific language arts standards. She can also work to deepen students' understanding of the text by asking them to draw on specific strategies that will help build their reading comprehension.

Chernelle's Classroom—The Gold Rush

Chernelle is a fourth-grade teacher in San Francisco, California. She designed the simulation below to deepen students' understandings around the Gold Rush in California.

After students have engaged in a choral reading about the Gold Rush from their textbooks, Chernelle instructs them to stack their textbooks in the middle of their desk clusters. She explains to them that they are miners of 1849 and will be doing a role-play activity. She gives them the following activity rules: "Your desks are your claims. Any gold you find on your claim is yours. Well, actually any gold you find *near* your claim is yours. . . . Well, actually any gold you find *anywhere* can be yours."

She explains to students that they should put themselves in the miners' shoes and imagine what it was like to be a miner. She states, "Everybody should be able to find gold. If any two students happen to both find gold at the same time, they must use one round of roshambo (rock-paper-scissors) to dispute or settle their disagreement peacefully and quickly."

Once the desks are separated, to emulate each miner's excavation site, Chernelle lightly tosses pennies, which represent the gold, onto the claim areas of the students. The students quickly gather all the gold that they can find.

After all the pennies are tossed, Chernelle asks the students to sit at their desks and count up their gold pieces. She then asks students to share how many pieces of gold they were able to find. Next, she tells the miners that unfortunately some "fool's gold" or fake look-a-like gold was in the land. She explains to students that pennies dated 1987 or older are real gold pieces. Pennies dated 1988 through 2012 are fool's gold. To assist students, Chernelle draws a large picture of a penny on the white board and maps out where they can find the year the penny was made. Chernelle also draws a time line to help her students differentiate between real gold and fool's gold. She then asks students again to report their individual number of real gold pieces.

After students share out, Chernelle asks her class to come to the carpet and think about the following questions: "How did you feel when the gold was tossed? How did you feel when someone took gold off your claim? How did you feel when you discovered you had some fool's gold and you were not as rich as you initially thought?" As a whole group, students shared their feelings around the role play and the emotions they felt during the activity.

After the discussion, Chernelle asks students to return to their desks and fill out the "L" section of their KWL chart with what they have *Learned* about the Gold Rush from the text and the role-play activity. Chernelle used the

"K" (What do you want to know?) in the first lesson to inspire wonder in her students. To assist students in filling out the L section of their graphic organizer, Chernelle writes guiding questions on the board such as: How did the Gold Rush travelers get to California? Describe the three travel routes. What materials did miners use? What are claims? Do you think mining was always fair? Why or why not?

In this excerpt, Chernelle uses simulation as a supplement to textbook reading. The language used in textbooks can often be quite cumbersome for students, especially English language learners. Moreover, because so many students find textbook readings so boring, the lack of engaging quality of the text also discourages many students from adequately comprehending the content. Additionally, the textbook often portrays only one perspective. Chernelle's simulation allows students to imagine what it was like for the miners during the Gold Rush. They can feel emotions such as greed, wealth, anger, and discouragement. They can also find empathy by experiencing other people's struggles. When expected to adhere to a mandated curriculum, using simulation as a complementary resource may really help your students engage with the text and better grasp social studies content.

Chernelle could expand on the simulation to portray multiple perspectives. For example, the discovery of gold in California attracted many different miners, including the Chinese who came to the country as free laborers. In 1852 a foreign miner's tax was enacted aimed directly at the Chinese. Although the Chinese contributed greatly to the construction of the Central Pacific Railroad and were vital contributors to the agricultural industry of California, the Chinese became targets of White labor resentment, especially during hard times (Takaki, 2008).

Many miners also came from Mexico, where techniques for extracting gold had been developed. Mexicans shared these techniques with White miners. In return, Whites resented the Mexicans as competitors, claiming that they had the "right" to the gold (Takaki, 2008). In both respects, the Chinese and Mexicans were used for their contributions and labor, but a heavy ceiling was set to prevent them from prospering in the country (e.g., taxes and unfair wages and working conditions). Although both groups proved essential in the building of our country, their stories are left unheard and silenced in our textbooks. As teachers teach about the Gold Rush, a common topic for California fourth-grade classrooms, an emphasis must be set on illuminating the complexity of the historical time period. Chernelle could adapt the simulation so that each student receives a role. Some students could be White miners wanting to keep all the gold for themselves, while other students could be Mexican miners trying to recover financially from the land they lost during the Mexican-American War. The Chinese miners could be in America after newly immigrating and share their experience of trying to find gold in a new land. By integrating multiple perspectives, students may begin to see that the Gold Rush did not only include White Americans. People of color were there and had stories to tell.

They fought for their rights when given unfair wages, and struggled to survive in a time and place where they were heavily discriminated against.

We also see Chernelle using a graphic organizer, the KWL chart, as a quick tool for assessment. She revised the third lesson of her unit based on her analysis of that assessment. By providing students with an opportunity to discuss after the role play, Chernelle could meet the following ELA Common Core Standards for Speaking and Listening, grade 4:

Connecting to Common Core State Standards
Comprehension and Collaboration
SL.4.1. Engage effectively in a range of collaborative discussions (one-on-one, in groups, and teacher-led) with diverse partners on grade 4 topics and texts, building on others' ideas and expressing their own clearly.

Role plays and simulations play an important function in social justice–oriented social studies education. They make social studies content more accessible to all of our learners and shed light on the complexity of historical events. In thinking of ways to teach social studies and literacy, role plays and simulations offer us opportunities to meet language arts Common Core Standards for Speaking and Listening. Students learn to build off each other's ideas, draw on their background knowledge, and express their understandings in light of what they have learned.

ARTIFACT ANALYSIS

As discussed in Chapter 2, in an artifact analysis students learn to examine evidence through investigatory techniques and critical thinking. Documents can serve as important pathways of information. Primary resources "help you and your students get as close as possible to what actually happened. They're artifacts of a certain time, created at the time being studied, by the people being studied" (Schmidt, 2007, p. 44). Primary documents include diaries, letters, autobiographies, memoirs, photographs, arrest records, eviction notices, advertisements, speeches, recipes, law ledgers, and newspapers. Secondary resources can also serve as a valuable set of information, when they analyze primary resources. Some important secondary resources include encyclopedias, the Internet, dictionaries, books, and articles. By presenting students with primary and secondary documents, teachers make the documents into learning resources (Sunal & Haas, 2008). Students have opportunities to critically examine the evidence presented to them (primary and secondary resources) and to make conclusions based on what they see.

While students are engaged in an artifact analysis, they are asking critical questions such as the following about the document presented to them:

- What is the document?
- Where is it from?
- Whom is the author writing the document for?
- Who benefits from the document? Who does not?
- What is the message being portrayed?
- What do the words say?
- What do you learn from the document?
- What does the author hope to do with this document?
- Why might the author have bias?
- Would you reform the document? How?

As students are examining the document, they are also learning an important reading comprehension strategy: making inferences. When we infer, we go beyond surface details to see other meanings that might be implied or suggested by the author. For example, if a text said "Mina brought her child to school," we have a simple statement about what someone did. When we unpack the sentence we begin to make inferences: (1) Mina is a woman, (2) Mina has a son or a daughter, and (3) Mina goes to the school. We may begin to widen our inference to think: (1) maybe Mina is a school teacher? or (2) maybe Mina brought her child to school because she cannot take her child to day care? As we make inferences while reading, we also do this when analyzing primary and secondary documents.

In addition to documents, we can also use illustrations as a resource for students to analyze. For example, Figure 3.1 is a good illustration to analyze when teaching about the Columbus and Taino encounter. I use the follow guiding questions:

- What do you see in this picture?
- Who is shown with power? Who is shown without?
- Why do you think this illustration was created?
- What was the artist's message?
- How are the natives portrayed in the picture?
- How are Columbus and his people portrayed?
- What else do you notice about the portrait?

Students work in their groups to critically analyze the picture. They make inferences based on their background knowledge and the evidence they can collect through the illustration. I supplement this illustration with a reading from Loewen's book *Lies My Teacher Told Me* (2007). For some students, the illustration, with the reading, disrupts their conception of Columbus as a heroic explorer. Many of my students are shocked and saddened to learn of the

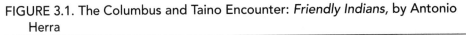

FIGURE 3.1. The Columbus and Taino Encounter: *Friendly Indians,* by Antonio Herra

atrocities Columbus and his men committed against the Taino people. This is key in social justice–oriented social studies teaching. Not only do we want students to gain a deep understanding of social studies content through the critical examination of multiple perspectives, but we also want to counter any misconceptions students may have learned through their textbooks, media, and so on.

Through artifact analysis, students have the opportunity to gather information for themselves, make inferences, and make assertions based on the evidence they collect. Letters, diaries, illustrations, and so forth are all excellent resources for helping students uncover the past and getting them to think critically about social studies content through the exploration of multiple perspectives.

Claire's Classroom—Farmworkers

We met Claire, a third-grade teacher in Oakland, in Chapter 2. In her first lesson, Claire used a personal story as a means to inspire wonder in her students about the Farmworkers Movement in 1965. As she continues with her unit, Claire works to deepen students' content knowledge by painting a picture for them of the working conditions of farmworkers prior to the United Farmworkers Movement.

To begin the lesson, Claire has students seated at their desks while she is at the front of the room with her projector and computer. She says to students, "Yesterday, I shared my story of peaceful protest. We also talked about the Farmworkers Movement and the struggles farmworkers faced. Today we will be learning about the working conditions and treatment of farmworkers prior to the Farmworkers Movement through a slide show of photographs from that time period." After stating her objective, Claire shows the slides to her students. She then asks her students to "think-pair-share" about what they saw. *Think-pair-share* is a strategy used to engage students in a quick discussion with a partner. The partner can be assigned in advance or students can think-pair-share with whoever is sitting closest to them. She writes the following questions on the board:

- Who did you see in the pictures?
- What did you learn about the treatment of the farmworkers?
- How would you feel if this were you or one of your family members?
- Do you think it is right to treat people this way?

After students share with their partners, she asks them to choose one of the questions listed on the board and do a "quick-write" for about 10 minutes. The focus during a quick-write is often not on correct writing structure or grammar, but rather an effort to get students critically reflecting. Sometimes, quick-writes are collected as a quick means of assessment, other times they are not collected and used to guide classroom discussion. Claire chose to collect the quick-writes for assessment purposes.

As students finish their quick-writes, she asks them to focus back to the front. In the next set of slides, Claire shows her students photographs of farmworkers protesting their conditions through marches, strikes, and boycotts. After students see the slides, Claire reviews the types of protest. Claire then introduces a graphic organizer to students in which they will be organizing information they learned about protests. Using a graphic organizer, students label their worksheet "Types of Protest" and write definitions with pictures of each type of protest they saw in the slide show. Claire shows students an action they could use to help them remember each type of protest. For example, for *march,* students got out of their chair and practiced marching.

To end the lesson, Claire asks her students to reflect on the following questions:

- How did the slide show help us understand how migrant farmworkers were treated?
- How did the photographs help us learn about peaceful protest?

- What did the farmworkers do to protest their working conditions?
- Do you think things have changed today?

In Claire's case, she uses photographs to paint a picture of migrant farmworkers' working conditions prior to the United Farmworkers Movement. She begins the lesson connecting to students' prior learning and making explicit the connection between yesterday's and today's lessons. She then uses a variety of photographs to portray the hardships and struggles farmworkers faced. She follows the first slide show with a second series of slides to show how the farmworkers peacefully protested for their rights. In this way, students do not only see how a group of people were oppressed, but they also see how a group collectively worked to make change for themselves and future generations through peaceful protest.

In our textbooks, the voice of migrant farmworkers may be minimally represented, if represented at all. If expected to adhere to a mandated curriculum, a teacher could use artifact analysis, just as Claire did, to show the perspective of the migrant farmworkers. When the perspective of the farmworkers is absent from the stories we tell of our nation's history, we silence the hardships and struggle of those who contributed greatly to our country's prosperity. Our migrant farmworkers, for example, greatly influenced the success and growth of our nation's agricultural production and collectively changed the path of treatment for farmworkers today.

In addition to deepening students' content understandings around the farmworkers movement, Claire used strategies specifically designed to support all learners in her classroom, especially her English language learners. For example, the slide show itself offers students opportunities to learn that are not just limited to readings from the text. Visual aids, such as the slide show, make the language and content more accessible to English language learners. Claire also uses a graphic organizer, which can be helpful to all students when learning how to organize information and ideas. She also has students work collaboratively in pairs during think-pair-share to encourage high-level thinking and to create a space where students may feel more comfortable responding to questions. Last, quick-writing is a great strategy to get students thinking freely without the restrictions of spelling and sentence structure.

If Claire did not have the time to enact the slide show during an explicit social studies period, she could integrate the slide show and lesson into her language arts time. She could use the slide show to build students' content knowledge about the Farmworkers Movement and as a minilesson to teach students about an important reading comprehension strategy, making inferences. At the beginning of the lesson, Claire could say, "Yesterday, I shared my story of peaceful protest. We also talked about the Farmworkers Movement and the struggles farmworkers faced. Today we will be learning about the working conditions and treatment of farmworkers prior to the Farmworkers Movement. We will be looking at slides and making inferences. Inference is an important reading comprehension strategy. When we infer, we read between the lines. We do this as readers, but we also do this as historians. When looking at the pictures, see what you can infer." As Claire continues with the lesson, she will challenge students to critically analyze the pictures and think about the perspectives of the migrant farmworkers, but she will continue to illuminate the word *inference* so students are also learning about an important comprehension strategy. She may follow up with the strategy of inference in her guided reading groups or during a read-aloud. By highlighting the reading comprehension strategy of inference in her lesson, Claire could meet the following ELA Common Core Standards for Speaking and Listening, grade 3:

Connecting to Common Core State Standards

SL.3.1. Engage effectively in a range of collaborative discussions (one-on-one, in groups, and teacher-led) with diverse partners on grade 3 topics and texts, building on others' ideas and expressing their own clearly.

As Claire teaches she has students draw on their prior knowledge and learning, thinking critically about the slides and documents presented to them, and using the reading comprehension strategy of inference to express ideas and understandings.

John's Classroom—The Great Depression

John is a fifth-grade teacher in San Francisco, California. To teach students about the Great Depression, John employs a visual thinking strategy whereby students study Dorothea Lange photographs and record their thoughts, relying only on information from the previous lesson to guide their interpretations of the photographs.

Prior to this lesson, John inspired wonder in his students by engaging them in a slide show and simulations that helped them see and experience some of the hardships people faced during the Great Depression. The purpose of the first lesson was to instill curiosity and build background knowledge to prepare students for the subsequent lessons in the unit.

To begin the lesson, John reads to his students the biography *Dorothea Lange: A Life Beyond Limits* (Gordon, 2009). Dorothea Lange was an influential artist and photographer, best known for her photographs humanizing the tragic consequences of the Great Depression. After reading the book, John divides the class into four groups to each analyze a photo taken by Lange. He informs students that Lange's photographs were published in newspapers and were accompanied with stories during the Great Depression. Each group receives a handout with the following questions to accompany the photograph they are asked to analyze:

- Who is in this picture?
- What can you say about the people you see in the photograph?
- What can you tell from the setting shown in the photograph?
- Where do you think the photographer was standing when she took the picture?
- How would you describe the mood of the image?
- How do you feel about the different images?
- How do you think Lange felt about the people she photographed? What makes you say that?
- Why do you think Lange took each photograph? What makes you say that?
- Could the photograph shown be in a newspaper related to a current event?
- What current event would the photograph represent?
- What would be different in the photograph if Lange had taken it today?
- What would a current headline read for the photograph?

After each group has the opportunity to analyze a photo, John pulls the class back together to discuss the photos as a whole group. One by one, he projects each photo on a big screen. Students who were assigned that photo share their reactions and ideas about it. Classmates also respond to the picture and share their ideas and beliefs.

At the end of the lesson, John ask his students why it's important to study people and photographs. He asks them, "What do we see in the photographs that we did not necessarily learn in our textbooks?" In subsequent lessons, John continues to deepen students' content knowledge on the Great Depression by engaging them in an application activity where they become journalists writing newspaper articles about the photographs they studied in this lesson. They then make connections to the past and present through a Venn-diagram activity where students compare and contrast the Great Depression with our current recession. The unit ends with the teacher facilitating action. To facilitate action, students write letters to their local congressperson about increasing unemployment and home foreclosures in their communities due to the current recession.

John uses photographs to get students thinking critically about the Great Depression and the people involved. He begins the lesson with a read-aloud, building students' background knowledge of the artist Dorothea Lange. Next, he connects the read-aloud to an artifact analysis by presenting students with photographs of the Great Depression taken by Lange. Like Claire, John integrates strategies specifically designed to support the English language learners in his classroom. The Venn diagram is used to help students compare and contrast the Great Depression with today's recession. In this way, students are making critical connections between the past and the present, but they are also learning to organize content in accessible ways. Through artifact analysis, John is engaging his students in a deep exploration of the Great Depression through the exploration of multiple perspectives while simultaneously encouraging his students to make connections between the financial hardships people faced in the past and the hardships of today.

If expected to adhere to a mandated curriculum, like Claire, John could use this activity to supplement the textbook. The slide show may offer perspectives and stories invisible in textbooks. The activity may also evoke emotion in students in a way that a textbook could not because of students' exposure to photos of real people and their stories. If John were limited in the time he could dedicate toward social studies, like Claire, he could illuminate the strategy of making inferences. He too could highlight the use of inference when analyzing a photograph and meet Common Core Standards for Speaking and Listening. Moreover, he could explain how inference allows us to make assertions about people and events based on the limited amount of evidence we have. John could transition the discussion around inference into his guided reading, shared reading, or independent reading.

In both examples, Claire and John use photographs to engage students in an artifact analysis. The teachers work to paint a picture for their students, one that is inclusive of multiple viewpoints and the struggles and resistance of people who lived during that time.

FILMS, FIELD TRIPS, AND GUEST SPEAKERS

When painting the picture, films, field trips, and guest speakers can be excellent resources for guiding students toward uncovering the past through multiple perspectives. Just like children's literature, these mediums for learning can offer a perspective that may be left invisible in textbooks. For example, the Great Depression (1929–1939) was the worst economic tragedy in America's history. Hundreds of thousands of people lost their jobs and homes, businesses went under, and financial institutions collapsed. To paint a picture for students of the Great Depression, we can lean on films, field trips, and guest speakers as a platform for sharing the stories of those who may remain unheard.

As White children and their families suffered through the Great Depression, people of color lost their jobs to unemployed Whites, even those jobs that were traditionally held by Blacks (e.g., busboys, cooks, maids). According to Wormser (2002), "a Klan-like group called the Black Shirts paraded carrying signs that read 'No jobs for niggers until every white man has a job.'" In addition to the discrimination people of color faced in regard to their employment, the Jim Crow laws continued to be enacted from 1876–1965. The laws mandated segregation in all public facilities, including public schools, public transportation, and public places, like restaurants. Although segregated facilities were supposed to be "separate but equal," most often the schools, restaurants, and bathrooms were in far worse condition than the facilities designated for Whites. Included in the Jim Crow laws was a denial for Blacks to vote and statutes passed by states that regulated social interactions between races.

The Great Depression was a complex time period for Americans, including children, White Americans, immigrants, and people of color. Our textbooks may sanitize the story of the Great Depression to only include hardships from a Eurocentric perspective and portray Roosevelt's New Deal as a magical antidote to the adversity people faced. Missing from the story may be the narrative of immigrants and Black Americans who struggled with discrimination and oppression during the time period or the stories of children who weren't given the opportunity to go to school, but rather were expected to work in factories because they could get jobs when the parents could not and so could provide food for the family. Our textbooks may also not include the story of women who sacrificed their own meals to feed their families.

To help integrate the narratives of others into the story of the Great Depression, organizations such as PBS (Public Broadcasting Service) provide a variety of videos named the *Jim Crow Stories* that illuminate the hardships of people of color during the Great Depression and prior to the Civil Rights Movement (Wormser, 2002). A visit to a history museum may allow you to share with students artifacts and realia from the Great Depression. A guest speaker may be hard to find, but is a valuable resource to share firsthand experiences of the Great Depression. Films, field trips, and guest speakers can help paint a vivid picture for students of the complexity behind historical events in our country and world. There are also a variety of websites that provide "virtual field trips." These field trips can offer great information to students as you paint the picture of what actually happened during this time. When using films or websites, be sure to preview them first for bias, content, and appropriateness.

Caroline's Classroom—The Constitution

Caroline is a fifth-grade teacher in San Francisco, California, who designed a unit plan to critically examine and understand the meaning of the United States Constitution through a social justice lens.

Caroline begins her lesson by writing the following quote on the board:

You may think that the Constitution is your security—it is nothing but a piece of paper. You may think that your statutes are security—but they are nothing but words in a book.

—Charles Evan Hughes, Chief Justice, U.S. Supreme Court

She then asks students to do a quick-write in their journals. She asks them the following questions: "Why are rules important?" and "Write one classroom rule/agreement that you agree with and explain why." After giving students a few minutes to respond, Caroline asks her students to think-pair-share with the person next to them. Caroline then calls on students to share their responses to the questions.

Caroline continues the conversation by having students think about how rules came about in their classroom. Caroline asks her students, "Why did we create our rules as a classroom community?" She then asks students, "Why do we have rules in our country? How is this similar or different from the reasons we have rules in our classroom?" After the discussion, Caroline explains that the Constitution was developed as a set of rules each American should follow to help our country run as a democracy. Amendments are additions and changes to the original rules.

Caroline then highlights some of the crucial content vocabulary on sentence strips that are put into a pocket chart at the front of the room. On each sentence strip is a word (e.g., *democracy, law, amendment,* and so on) with a corresponding definition. After Caroline has reviewed the vocabulary with her students, she explains to them that she will be showing a short video about the first amendment.

When the video is finished, Caroline asks students to do another think-pair-share. This time, they are required to teach the person next to them one piece of information they learned from the video. She then presents to students a graphic organizer. The first column is labeled *what we learned from the video.* The second column is labeled *what else do we want to know?*

Caroline ends the lesson reviewing important vocabulary and discussing the first amendment. She writes the first amendment on the board and asks her students to circle and color words they think are important. She then has students break out into groups to create posters that illustrate all of the five freedoms discussed in the first amendment. In later lessons, Caroline explores the following questions about the Constitution using the framework presented in this book:

- Who wrote the words? Who gets to decide what words are in the document?
- What happens when you don't agree with the words?
- What happens if those words don't protect you?
- What happens if those words don't protect others? What can you do?

Through this lesson Caroline wants her students to critically examine and understand the United States Constitution. She wants her students to be able to break apart the Constitution and understand what the words mean and why the words are meaningful. To inspire wonder, she asks them to question and think about the quote written on the front board. This quote undergirds the entire unit on the Constitution, as this unit, to Caroline, is about steering away from the more traditional curriculum presented in textbooks. So the unit is not focused primarily on the memorization of facts, names, and dates, but instead is focused on getting students to examine the Constitution from a social justice perspective.

To make learning accessible for students, Caroline leans on multiple strategies such as collaborative learning, think-pair-share, and graphic organizers. She also takes a large chunk of the lesson to review important content vocabulary that is necessary to know when reading the Constitution. By taking the time to unpack important vocabulary, Caroline can meet the following ELA Common Core Standards for Reading: Informational Text, grade 5:

Connecting to Common Core State Standards
Craft and Structure
RI.5.4. Determine the meaning of general academic and domain-specific words and phrases in a text relevant to a grade 5 topic or subject area.

Caroline can meet this standard through her lesson, as she is taking intentional steps to highlight key vocabulary and engage students in discussion and activities that challenge them to critically examine the words within the Constitution.

If expected to adhere to a mandated curriculum, Caroline could have students read an excerpt from their textbook to help build their background knowledge and then use the above lesson to supplement the textbook reading. After enacting her lesson, she could ask students these questions:

- What did you learn in this lesson that was not in the textbook?
- Why do you think this information was not in your textbook?
- Do you think your textbook would ask you the question I did: "What happens if the words in the amendment don't protect you?" Why or why not?
- Whose perspective does the textbook give us? Whose does it not?
- What else do you hope to learn about the Constitution?

By asking questions such as the ones listed above, Caroline can help her students see the bias in their textbooks and also get them thinking critically about texts like the U.S. Constitution. She can also adhere to the administration's requirement of following a mandated curriculum while maintaining her own commitment to teach for social justice.

If Caroline could not find time to teach social studies, she could easily teach this lesson during language arts. In this lesson Caroline is doing vocabulary work (highlighting important content vocabulary) and teaching students important reading comprehension strategies such as synthesizing, determining importance, and making connections. She could choose one of these strategies to focus on specifically during her lesson. She could reinforce the strategy during guided reading and read-alouds.

Kelsey's Classroom—Pre-Columbian Life

Kelsey is a fourth-grade teacher in San Francisco, California. She designed a unit plan to study pre-Columbian daily life in California. She asked an Ohlone man to come in and share his experiences as a means to paint a picture from the perspective of the Ohlone people.

Prior to this lesson, students read a chapter in their textbooks about pre-Columbian native life in California. She divided the class into groups and assigned each group a topic to research on life prior to Spanish colonization: relationship to land/nature, clothing/body decoration, structure of settlements, food/cooking, and arts and crafts. Students used their textbooks and supplementary texts to write a summary of their findings to share with the rest of the class.

On the day of this lesson, Kelsey invites a guest speaker of Ohlone descent to come and speak with the students about the traditions and customs of the Ohlone people. Kelsey asks the guest speaker to talk about his experience as an Ohlone and the experiences of his ancestors during the mission period. The guest speaker shares how the life of his people changed with colonization. Students also have the opportunity to ask the guest questions.

After the guest leaves, Kelsey engages students in a simulation to further deepen their understandings around pre-Columbian life. She wants students to experience the concept of change and what it feels like to have change inflicted on you. To begin the simulation, Kelsey removes all chairs, pencils, markers, and clipboards from the room. She then passes out small brown bags for each student to put their writing supplies in. After all writing utensils are removed, Kelsey gives each student a paper plate with a mechanical pencil lead. She tells students, "I want you to write me a report that describes the changes from a hunter-gatherer economy to an agricultural economy. You must only use the materials I provided you. This is the way things are going to be around here now."

Students try but find it impossible to write with a piece of lead. After a few minutes, Kelsey gathers her students together to discuss their experience. She asks them, "What was it like to do a familiar task in an unfamiliar way? How did you feel being forced to do this? What connections can you make between this simulation and the experiences of the natives during the mission period?"

Kelsey ends the lesson with her KWL graphic organizer. She asks students to fill out the "L" section of her chart. (The first two sections were filled out after the textbook activity.) Kelsey uses the KWL as an assessment.

By engaging students in a discussion after the guest speaker's talk and simulation, Kelsey meets the following ELA Common Core Standards for Speaking and Listening, grade 4:

Connecting to Common Core State Standards

Comprehension and Collaboration

SL.4.1. Engage effectively in a range of collaborative discussions (one-on-one, in groups, and teacher-led) with diverse partners on grade 4 topics and texts, building on others' ideas and expressing their own clearly.

Pose and respond to specific questions to clarify or follow up on information, and make comments that contribute to the discussion and link to the remarks of others.
Review the key ideas expressed and explain their own ideas and understanding in light of the discussion.

Through discussion, Kelsey offers her students opportunities to reflect on the simulation and guest speaker's talk. She poses questions to her students that challenge them to draw on their prior learning to gain a deeper understanding of the experiences for Natives at the missions.

When using guest speakers, we must be careful to not assume that one perspective is the same for all. Therefore, we must remind students that this was one person's experience and his or her experience may not be the same as all members of the group or tribe. For example, as an Indian woman, I can share with you my experiences, but I do not know the experiences of all Indian people. Given this, guest speakers can still be a valuable resource for students. Students get to hear history from someone's firsthand experience and experience empathy and emotion. In one sixth-grade world history class, a student's grandfather came to speak about the Holocaust. In his story he shared, detail by detail, descriptions of the containment camp and his escape. This man's story deeply affected many students. It made them more interested in learning about the Holocaust and also instilled a sense of injustice that angered and drove them to desire change.

In Kelsey's lesson, her guest speaker shared his story of the experience his people faced during the mission period and the changes that were forced on them, despite their own traditions and beliefs. Kelsey's simulation offered students the opportunity to see what life was like when change was inflicted on you, regardless of your own principles and ways of doing things. When engaged in the simulation, students may be able to empathize with some of the feelings and emotions natives faced when forced and expected to do things a certain way. Students might feel frustration, anger (that they could do this better and easier if they were only allowed to), and resentment.

Kelsey's use of multiple modalities to help her students access learning proves useful especially when considering the multiple ways students learn: Some students learn best visually, while others learn better through listening, doing, or teaching.

If expected to adhere to a mandated curriculum, this lesson could serve as a great supplement, allowing students to see the pre-Columbian perspective from the Ohlone people's point of view. The oppression and discriminatory practices the Ohlone people faced during this time period and after may not be illuminated in textbooks. A significant amount of time is required to teach this lesson. Therefore, a Friday afternoon that may be less structured may be a good time. It is difficult to translate this lesson into language arts, but key content vocabulary, which needs to be covered, could be taught during word work or vocabulary development. Kent and Simpson (2008) argue that "learning Social Studies vocabulary is critically linked to comprehending Social Studies content" (p. 145). By previewing social studies vocabulary during language arts, students will have the vocabulary they need to access the content presented to them during social studies. Therefore, teachers can reinforce the vocabulary during their social studies lesson, but focus the lesson primarily on teaching students content, as the vocabulary was already covered during the language arts period earlier in the day.

When painting the picture, films, field trips, and guest speakers can offer students great insight into the past and also provide opportunities for students to explore multiple perspectives. As teachers, we must be cognizant of the perspective the film, field trips, or guest speaker may present and make explicit to students that each historical account is only a partial story. We can expand on what may be presented in the film, field trips, and guest speakers through children's literature, primary and secondary sources, and even our textbook. Our goal is to scaffold learning for our students so that they may uncover the past through the exploration of multiple perspectives.

CONCLUSION

The purpose of painting the picture is for students to think critically about the past through the exploration of multiple perspectives. To do this, we challenge students to explore their misconceptions around history, critically question the bias in text, and examine points of view that may be silenced or limited in textbooks. This tenet, in particular, is designed to get students thinking deeply and critically about social studies content.

As we explore the past through multiple perspectives, students come to grapple with history and decide for themselves what really happened. A teacher may use any variety of the strategies listed in this section. Each of the strategies requires a teacher to look outside the box to find resources that speak to a perspective that may be silenced in textbooks. By allowing the voices of those silenced to enter the mainstream narrative, students may see history in a different light. They may get to hear the stories of people who are like them and their struggle to overcome discrimination and racism. They may hear about their ancestors' acts of resistance toward unfair practices and wages and also of their contribution to our country's growth. They may also learn from stories of children, like Ruby Bridges, whose bravery and courage impacted change in our country. Last, they may hear of those who used their privilege and resources to serve as allies and support systems to those struggling to obtain freedom and rights. In each case, students may feel inspired and empowered to hear the stories of members of our society who fought against discrimination, racism, and oppression to make change in our world. Through the exploration of multiple perspectives, students may see that our country was built by the complex contributions of many people, not just the ones listed in our textbooks. Moreover, the stories of those who contributed to our country may not just be limited to stories of happiness and victory, but stories entangled with hardship, fear, anger, distrust, and worry. Our history is not a sanitized list of facts, but a complex and dynamic story that worked to give power to some and deny power to others.

Textbooks can also serve as valuable tools to help paint the picture. They can help students gain background information about the event, and the illustrations, photographs, and documents presented in textbooks can be used for an artifact analysis activity. When presenting information in textbooks, it is essential that we challenge our students to ask critical questions about the text so that they may be aware of bias. If we choose to only present the Eurocentric viewpoint present in textbooks, we prohibit our students from understanding history from multiple perspectives and seeing the struggles and contributions of people who helped create this nation. The textbook can serve as a tool for helping students gain one perspective, see the bias in curriculum, examine photographs and documents, and compare and contrast viewpoints.

REFLECTION EXERCISES

Below are reflection exercises to help extend these concepts into classroom practice:

1. Consider the next lesson in social studies you are planning to teach.
    a. How could you paint the picture for your students so that you could include multiple perspectives?
    b. What resources would you use to help you?
    c. What strategies would you integrate into your lesson?
    d. How could you integrate language arts?
    e. What language arts Common Core Standards could you meet for your grade level?
2. If you are limited to using mandated curriculum in your classroom, how might you get your students thinking about the bias in their textbooks? What questions would you ask?
3. How would you challenge students' misconceptions around history? What are ways in which you could paint a picture for students of what really happened?
4. What are ways in which you could include stories of resistance? Why is it important to include stories of resistance in our social studies lesson plans?

CHAPTER 4

Application

URING INSPIRING WONDER and painting the picture, students are gathering a myriad of information they must learn to synthesize and understand, including information from textbooks, simulations, read-alouds, primary and secondary resources, and so on. Students must sift through complex social studies content to actively create interpretations of history for themselves. In application, students process and synthesize social justice–oriented social studies content.

In application, students piece together a historical puzzle based on their explorations and interpretations of history. Students also develop and share their own theories of what they believe happened in history based on their examination of multiple perspectives.

As we discuss spaces for application in this chapter, we will also discuss strategies you can use to provide a space for students to process and synthesize content knowledge. Each strategy shared will be supported with examples of teacher practice. Like previous chapters, we will also discuss how you can connect social studies content to language arts, meet language arts Common Core Standards, and lean on mandated curricular materials to find space to integrate the strategies discussed in this chapter. In this next section, we will discuss an important aspect of application, synthesis.

SYNTHESIZING SOCIAL STUDIES CONTENT

In application, we provide a space for our students to synthesize social studies content. Synthesizing is an important reading comprehension strategy (discussed in the previous chapter), as well as an important critical thinking strategy for interpreting social studies content. Keene and Zimmerman (2007) refer to synthesis as "the mind constructing beautiful mosaics of meaning . . . a meaning greater than the sum of each shiny piece" (p. 228). In this regard, synthesis relates to the complex process of piecing together numerous details to construct a meaning that is comprised of both our past and present learning. In other words, the ability to synthesize means to combine into a single understanding.

Our young learners often synthesize while reading. *Synthesis*, in connection to language arts, "is the sum of information from the text, other relevant texts, and the reader's background knowledge, ideas, and opinions, and may be produced or shared in an original way" (Keene & Zimmerman, 2007, p. 244). As students read, they synthesize by drawing on the information in their current texts, previous texts they've read, and their lived experience to construct and apply knowledge in a unique way. For example, young readers may use synthesis to draw a picture that reflects what they read or write a summary of the book. Proficient readers may use synthesis to share, recommend, and critically review books they have read (Keene & Zimmerman, 2007). As a reading comprehension strategy, synthesis helps students process and apply information so that they can better understand what they have read.

Allowing a space for students to process and apply new content information is important for all of our learners, especially our English language learners. By having students engage and practice new content in meaningful, concrete experiences, students can apply new knowledge and concepts. As Echevarria, Vogt, & Short (2004) note, "students have a greater chance of mastering concepts and skills when they are given multiple opportunities to practice in relevant, meaningful ways" (p. 119). These authors give different examples of spaces for application including clustering, using graphic organizers, solving problems in cooperative learning groups, writing in a journal, or engaging in discussion circles.

In this tenet of the framework, application, the strategies, with examples of teacher practice, demonstrate how to help students apply and process new information gathered from delving beneath the surface of traditional textbook content. As students process and synthesize new content information, they also formulate for themselves historical narratives inclusive of the perspectives not necessarily heard in our textbooks. Thus, in the application tenet of the framework, students should have opportunities to share their understandings of history, as well as to synthesize information gathered through the exploration of multiple perspectives. Additionally, students should have opportunities throughout the lesson to deconstruct and examine bias both in themselves and in the texts that surround them. In consequence, students may push past the bias normalized in traditional curriculum to form a historical narrative that is more inclusive of others' perspectives, ideas, and values.

WRITERS' WORKSHOP

In a comprehensive literacy program we address essential components of literacy through research-based teaching methods. Writers' Workshop can be an important piece of a comprehensive literacy program. It's a scheduled space in the day for students to develop their writing fluency and love for writing. Writers' Workshop, in conjunction with social studies, can also serve as an important space for students to process content information and apply their new

---

Connecting to Common Core State Standards

Text Types and Purposes

Write arguments to support claims in an analysis of substantive topics or texts, using valid reasoning and relevant and sufficient evidence.
Write informative/explanatory texts to examine and convey complex ideas and information clearly and accurately through the effective selection, organization, and analysis of content.
Write narratives to develop real or imagined experiences or events using effective technique, well-chosen details, and well-structured event sequences.

Production and Distribution of Writing

Produce clear and coherent writing in which the development, organization, and style are appropriate to task, purpose, and audience.
Develop and strengthen writing as needed by planning, revising, and editing, rewriting, or trying a new approach.
Use technology, including the Internet, to produce and publish writing and to interact and collaborate with others.

Research to Build and Present Knowledge

Draw evidence from literary or informational texts to support analysis, reflection, and research.

---

themselves an understanding of what they believed may have happened in history.

DIALOGUE POEMS

Poetry can serve as an important outlet for students to apply and process content knowledge. Writing in the genre of poetry can be academically rigorous, as well as dynamic and explorative. As poetry is often written in a flexible format, students have an opportunity to explore their ideas and thoughts about social studies content through a medium that may not be as constricting as a formal essay or pencil-and-paper test. As Christensen (2009) notes, "Poetry levels the writing playing field. . . . Poetry unleashes their [students] verbal dexterity—it's break dancing for the tongue" (p. 14). Because poetry does not require the same grammatical and structural constraints as other genres of writing, a student may be more willing to use poetry as a platform for application. Poetry provides a flexibility in writing and thinking that is unique compared to other more structured forms of writing.

The purpose of dialogue poems is for students to have a safe space to apply and process content knowledge. In a dialogue poem a pair of students juxtapose two different perspectives to create a poem that intersects and diverges with the unique thoughts of two different people. In short, students are developing a poem that shares the narratives of two people who may think very differently. Using this activity, teachers may challenge students to explore the conflicting viewpoints about issues such as gay rights, war, isolation of elderly people, or isolation of immigrants (Sleeter, 2005).

For a dialogue poem, two students work together and select two different points of view. Dialogue poems are "effective to use where controversy or different opinions might arise" (Burant, Christensen, Salas, & Walters, 2010, p. 197). The poems can also point out similarities between two people who might not seem to have much in common. Dialogue poems can be an especially powerful strategy to get students to understand multiple perspectives and empathize with those who have different life experiences. In social studies, teachers can also use this activity to explore conflicting and multiple viewpoints and reveal the voices of those who may not always be heard in our social studies textbooks.

In my social studies course students are asked to write a dialogue poem to juxtapose the Taino perspective with the perspective of Columbus and his men. Prior to this activity (during the painting the picture portion of the unit), students engaged in an in-depth study of the Taino and Columbus encounter, including participation in simulations, reviewing children's picture books, and reading books about the Taino people and excerpts from Christopher Columbus's journal. The purpose of these activities was to illustrate the encounter between the natives and Columbus and his men from the Taino perspective. After engaging in these activities, students created Venn diagrams to help them see the conflicts and convergences between the two perspectives.

Graphic organizers, such as a Venn diagram, serve as a great support structure for all learners in the classroom, especially English language learners. Graphic organizers can be effective tools for helping young writers organize their thinking and writing (Scharer & Pinnell, 2008) and help students interpret texts. Graphic organizers can also help students develop higher level thinking and promote creativity. In the case of the dialogue poem the Venn diagram was used to help students compare and contrast perspectives. Providing students a space to organize information and their thoughts is an important way for students to apply and process content knowledge.

When teaching students how to write a dialogue poem, a model that students can be given to structure their poems is the ABC format, which can be taught during a minilesson. In the example provided below, the students replaced the ABC with BCT to make it clearer for themselves who spoke when. Venn diagrams and reading materials at the front of the room can be helpful resources for students. It is good to remind students to think about where the perspectives conflict, but also where they converge, as we all have strengths and weaknesses in our viewpoints. Each poem is published and celebrated at the end of class. For our young writers or English language learners, we could have students draw out a dialogue poem. To draw a dialogue poem, students fold a piece of paper in half and draw the perspective of one person on one side and the perspective of the other person on the second half of the paper. Students can then label their drawings with a sentence describing how each person felt.

Below is a poem developed by two of my students. B stands for both, C for Christopher Columbus, and T for Taino.

B   I am a person.
C   I am Christopher Columbus, I will always be remembered.
T   I am Taino, I am easily forgotten.

B   I live on this planet.
C   I found a new world.
T   My world is ancient.

B   I am a good person.
C   God sent me to save the heathen.
T   I value kindness and generosity.

B   I believe in the sacred.
C   God ordained my journey.
T   My Gods display themselves in food, water, and fertility.

B   I submit to authority.
C   My divine Queen gives me her blessing.
T   I answer to my chief.

B   I fight.
C   I use my might to prove my point.
T   I outfox my enemies to take their weapons.

B   How will you remember me?

Poetry can serve as a medium for students to process and grapple with the large amounts of information they received in previous lessons. Dialogue poems, in particular, allow students to examine multiple perspectives and investigate how the ideas of two different groups or people may collide and connect.

As poetry is often a genre that must be covered in the year, teachers can integrate social studies content into language arts. A teacher may follow a Writers' Workshop format, giving students ample time to draft their thoughts and ideas. If a Writers' Workshop model is followed and students have the opportunity to plan, revise, edit, and publish their writing, teachers can meet Common Core Anchor Standards for Writing such as the following:

Connecting to Common Core State Standards

Production and Distribution of Writing

- Produce clear and coherent writing in which the development, organization, and style are appropriate to task, purpose, and audience.
- Develop and strengthen writing as needed by planning, revising, and editing, rewriting, or trying a new approach.
- Use technology, including the Internet, to produce and publish writing and to interact and collaborate with others.

By allowing students to move through the writing process before publishing their final poems, teachers can meet language arts Common Core Standards and create a space for students to synthesize, apply, and process critical social studies content.

Teachers who have to lean on mandated curriculum structures could also use textbooks as a resource for students to obtain additional knowledge. Whenever turning to the textbook, teachers should remind their students that this is just one source of knowledge from one point of view. Perhaps a student could compare and contrast the perspective of someone represented in the textbook during the California Gold Rush (White, European, male miners) with someone silenced in traditional curriculum (Chinese females).

If a teacher is limited with time, this lesson could be taught in one day. Students could draft their poems in class and finish their final drafts for homework. This is not ideal, but still allows for space for students to apply and process content knowledge. The celebration of writing allows students to be proud of their writing and also provides an opportunity for one to learn from the other.

FIRST PERSON NARRATIVE

A first person narrative is a record or account narrated by one author who speaks about herself or himself. Examples of first person narratives include diaries, journals, travel journals, memories, autobiographies, or oral histories.

First person narratives are a unique form of writing, in that one becomes the historical character in a story. A student must deeply understand the experiences of the individual person he or she chooses to write about. For example, if Carlos wanted to write a journal entry from the perspective of a Chinese miner during the Gold Rush period, he would need to explore large amounts of information to be able to thoughtfully portray the miner's perspective. To write a narrative, students need to draw on prior learning and possibly conduct some new research to adequately portray another's lived experiences.

As students learn and write about specific historical figures, students may gain empathy, awareness, and/or sensitivity toward the feelings, experiences, and thoughts of others. As Schmidt (2007) explains, "students can relate to people who are lonely, frustrated, trying to solve a problem, or celebrating triumph" (p. 90). As humans, we individually and collectively experience emotions. If we willingly share our feelings, we may find seeds of similarity that connect us in ways that may have previously served to separate us. By having students write narratives from the perspective of historical figures, we offer our students the opportunity to empathize with and learn from someone who may see things from a different perspective.

In the Writers' Workshop

In Writers' Workshop, a teacher can introduce the genre of narrative writing through a minilesson. In the minilesson, we can show examples of different types of narratives, including journals, letters, memoirs, and autobiographies. For English language learners, it may be helpful to find first person documents in a student's primary language. Examples of first person narratives can be pulled from the Internet or social studies textbooks, which often include first person documents that teachers can integrate into their lessons.

After exposing students to different types of narratives, students choose which form of narrative they wish to use to process and apply their content knowledge. For example, a student wishing to write from the perspective of an African American soldier during the Civil War may decide that a diary entry is the best way to share his ideas, while a student hoping to express the journey of a woman activist during the Civil Rights Movement might feel that her ideas are best portrayed through a memoir. Other times, a teacher may choose the form of the first person narrative; for example, a teacher may decide that all students will write a journal entry from the perspective of an Asian immigrant during the Gold Rush.

When beginning their writing process, the following questions may help students during their prewriting stage:

- What type of document is this?
- When and where was the document written?
- Who is the author?
- What is the author's age, interest, and education?
- What type of person is the author?

- Why is the author writing a journal, letter, memoir, or other writing?
- Is the author writing for herself or himself or for others?
- Who do you think is the audience?
- Does the author have a specific message?
- What primary and secondary resources will I lean on to help me write my narrative?
- Will I need to do more research?
- What do I need to remember?
- What emotions do I want to reveal?
- Who do I want to talk to?
- How will I structure my writing?
- What examples of writing can I use to help me?

Questions like the ones listed above may help students construct a vision of their historical character, determine what format they will use (e.g., letter, diary, other), and push students to think about what resources will help them.

Teaching narrative writing through a Writers' Workshop process lends itself to meeting many Common Core Anchor Standards for Writing including:

Connecting to Common Core State Standards

Text Types and Purposes

- Write narratives to develop real or imagined experiences or events using effective technique, well-chosen details, and well-structured event sequences.

Production and Distribution of Writing

- Produce clear and coherent writing in which the development, organization, and style are appropriate to task, purpose, and audience.
- Develop and strengthen writing as needed by planning, revising, and editing, rewriting, or trying a new approach.
- Use technology, including the Internet, to produce and publish writing and to interact and collaborate with others.

Research to Build and Present Knowledge

- Draw evidence from literary or informational texts to support analysis, reflection, and research.

Through narrative writing a teacher can explicitly teach her students the components of a narrative, how to organize and address an audience, and how to draw on evidence from informational texts to support one's writing. In this way, a teacher can meet many language arts Common Core Standards and engage students in an activity which allows them to process and synthesize social studies content.

Writing in narrative format allows students to express themselves in a medium that may not be as constricting as a formal essay. The emotion and passion that is immersed in the stories our students write may work to build community, as well as provide opportunities for students to deeply connect with social studies content.

Chernelle's Classroom—The Gold Rush

We met Chernelle, a fourth-grade teacher in San Francisco, in the previous chapter. She designed a unit on the Gold Rush in California. Her objective was for students to explore and examine the Gold Rush era from multiple perspectives. She painted a picture for her students of the Gold Rush through simulations, textbook readings, primary documents (e.g., photographs of mining sites), and read-alouds such as the book *The California Gold Rush* (Uschan, 2002).

Chernelle begins this lesson by giving her students one minute to discuss among their table groups what they found to be the most interesting fact about the California Gold Rush. She then asks her students, "What might be another group that was affected by the Gold Rush?" After students share, she continues, "Today we will focus on another group that was deeply affected by the Gold Rush, the Native Americans." She asks students to join her in a choral reading from their textbook. After finishing the choral reading, Chernelle reads excerpts to her students from *The Miwok of California* (Williams, 2005) which describes the destruction of the forests and streams by miners who disregarded the sacred land of the native Miwok and their ancestors. After finishing the reading, Chernelle asks her students:

- How do you think the Miwok felt when the gold miners arrived and took their land?
- Why do you think the miners called the Miwok names?
- How did mining affect how the Miwok supported themselves in regard to hunting, fishing, and gathering?

Following the discussion Chernelle reads aloud a brief account, written by army lieutenant Phillip H. Sheridean in 1855 from the book *The Fools of '49: The California Gold Rush, 1848–1856* (Seidman, 1976). The account describes the lieutenant's observation of the Native American group's struggle to find food due to the mining efforts. Mining efforts also resulted in many Native Americans losing their homes and land, being captured as slaves, killed, and cheated in unfair trades. After Chernelle finishes the short reading, she guides students through the following discussion questions:

- What do you think happens to fish when rivers get dammed or water is drawn from them for hydraulic mining purposes?
- How did these mining factors affect Native Americans?
- How do you feel about the antihydraulic mining law after hearing how it affected the Native Americans?
- If you lived back then, how would you help the land or the Native Americans?

Chernelle continues her lesson by telling students to pretend that they live in the era of the California Gold Rush. She explains, "We have the opportunity to help the land and the Native Americans by writing a letter to the United States government urging them to make a law to stop hydraulic mining. Together we will brainstorm reasons why hydraulic mining is bad for the environment and for Native Americans. I will write these reasons on the board." After the class has brainstormed reasons why hydraulic mining is destructive, Chernelle models for her students how to write a formal letter and posts the model letter frame at the front of the class to help scaffold English language learners in their writing process.

Students then take out their social studies journals and write their letters independently. She reminds students that they are required to write how mining has affected the environment and how it has affected the daily lives of California Native Americans in their letter to the United States government. She also encourages students to use the brainstorming ideas that are posted at the front of the class.

To recap, Chernelle begins her lesson by drawing on students' prior knowledge and explicitly stating the objective of her lesson. Through the read-alouds and discussion, she builds students' background knowledge about the Miwok Indians, including students' understanding of the consequences to the Miwok's land during the Gold Rush period. To support her students through the activity, she provides graphic organizers, visuals, and sentence frames. These tools may be especially helpful to English language learners in the classroom.

Chernelle also engages her students in a letter-writing activity, which she models prior to having her students write independently. Her framing of the letter is especially important because it encourages students to engage in a letter-writing assignment designed to promote social change. Students are writing about the Miwok Indians from a capacity perspective, where the Miwok Indians are portrayed as powerful and energized to make change in their communities.

Through this lesson, Chernelle is able to meet Common Core Standards for both Speaking and Listening and Writing. Through the read-alouds and discussion, she meets the ELA Common Core Standards for Speaking and Listening, grade 4, on the following page.

Also, if Chernelle explicitly teaches her students how to introduce their ideas and support them with evidence in a formal letter format, Chernelle most likely could meet these ELA Common Core Standards for Writing, grade 4:

Connecting to Common Core State Standards

Comprehension and Collaboration

SL.4.1. Engage effectively in a range of collaborative discussions (one-on-one, in groups, and teacher-led) with diverse partners on grade 4 topics and texts, building on others' ideas and expressing their own clearly.

Connecting to Common Core State Standards

Text Types and Purposes

W.4.1. Write opinion pieces on topics or texts, supporting a point of view with reasons and information.
- Introduce a topic or text clearly, state an opinion, and create an organizational structure in which related ideas are grouped to support the writer's purpose.
- Provide reasons that are supported by facts and details.
- Link opinion and reasons using words and phrases.
- Provide a concluding statement or selection related to the opinion presented.

Through Chernelle's lesson, we can see how she enacted a social justice–oriented lesson by providing students the chance to learn about the Gold Rush from a perspective that is often minimized in our textbooks. By drawing on supplementary materials and providing spaces for students to discuss and reflect, she was able to offer her students critical social studies content and also meet Common Core language arts Standards for Speaking and Listening. Chernelle was also able to meet Common Core language arts Standards for Writing by engaging students in a letter-writing activity that allowed them to synthesize and process their prior learning around the Gold Rush.

If a teacher could allot more time to the lesson, she could walk students through the narrative writing in a slower process. Students would have time to prewrite, draft, revise, edit, and publish their writing. After all students complete their first person narratives, a celebration could take place to honor their hard work and efforts. Minilessons could be taught over the course of the workshop to teach dialogue, description, and figurative language. This increases students' knowledge as writers and also allows teachers to meet more of the Common Core Standards for Writing that they need to cover for language arts.

During the independent writing portion of Writers' Workshop, a teacher could meet with individual students or groups to help them with specific needs.

DRAMATIZATION AND VISUAL ART

For many of our students who are artistically inclined or who may not yet be comfortable expressing themselves by speaking or writing, visual orientations such as art and performance can offer students an important space to synthesize new content knowledge (Perry & Fraser, 1993).

Visual representations, such as collages, offer our students a medium to express themselves in a way that does not rely on written language. Levstik and Barton (2005) explain:

> The very process of selecting representations for their inner conceptions shapes students' historical understandings. Whereas otherwise students might have relied largely on written language to convey ideas, they now have a wider repertoire of forms and symbols available to them. (p. 200)

Students, especially our English language learners, may be better able to make their inner ideas and conceptions more public if we provide them with a wider repertoire of forms and symbols to engage with. For example, a teacher asks her students to write a letter about the Chinese Exclusion Act from the perspective of a Chinese immigrant. A student with limited English proficiency may find it difficult to apply what he has learned about the Chinese Exclusion act through a letter-writing format, but may find an artistic format, such as a collage, a meaningful way to convey the same ideas without the structure and language needed to adequately write a letter. To build his collage, a student may collect photographs of the Chinese coming to America and print out poems that were written by the Chinese detained during the Chinese Exclusion Act to paste on his collage. In addition, the student might draw pictures in the collage that express the emotions of the struggle and hardships Chinese faced during this time. Through this activity, a student may be able to illustrate his interpretation of a historical event in a way that is meaningful to him. For a beginning English learner, visual art and dramatization may be a more viable space for synthesizing content than in a more structured written format. Students could also create murals and drawings that show their historical interpretations and understandings.

Through visual art, a teacher can meet Common Core Anchor Standards for Speaking and Listening if the teacher offers her students the opportunity to share and discuss their work. Some of the standards a teacher might cover include the standards outlined on the next page.

A teacher could meet either of the Common Core Anchor Standards on page 90 by offering students opportunities to collaborate and share their work

---

Connecting to Common Core State Standards

Comprehension and Collaboration

- Prepare for and participate effectively in a range of conversations and collaborations with diverse partners, building on others' ideas and expressing their own clearly and persuasively.

Presentation of Knowledge and Ideas

- Make strategic use of digital media and visual displays of data to express information and enhance understanding of presentations.

---

with others. Working collaboratively provides students the chance to develop their beliefs, ideas, and interpretations based on evidence they have collected through activities and readings. Debate with others may increase a student's ability to reason and think critically about social studies content.

Creating a Tableau

A group of students could also apply their content knowledge by creating a tableau. A tableau is an activity where a group of students physically constructs a scene from a historical event using body placement, facial expressions, and sometimes props.

When creating a tableau, a group begins their discussion identifying a scene, its importance, and from whose perspective the scene will be created. Teachers could encourage their students to choose a perspective that may be silenced or limited in their textbooks. For example, if students just finished a study of World War II, a group of students may decide to create a tableau illustrating the internment camps along the Pacific coast of the United States from the perspective of a Japanese American child. Following the attack on Pearl Harbor, President Franklin D. Roosevelt issued an executive order permitting the mass incarceration of those with as little as 1/16 Japanese blood (Takaki, 2008).

Once the scene is determined, students lean on their prior knowledge and what they've learned from prior lessons to help them understand what they know and what they still need to learn. Students might use a graphic organizer, such as a web, to organize their information. Teachers may encourage students to turn to primary and secondary resources, such as journal entries, to better understand the feelings, emotions, and struggles associated with the topic being studied. After all of the information has been collected and synthesized, students begin planning their performance. In this instance, the "freeze frame" created by this particular group of students depicts a scene of a child separated from his family holding a sign saying "one-drop."

Through tableau, students are expressing their conceptions of social studies content through a medium other than writing and speaking and also engaging in a space to synthesize, apply, and expand their historical interpretations.

As a teacher, it's important to remember that art and performance hold bias and valued interpretations just as writing and speaking do. We can challenge our students to examine art and performance for bias by asking questions such as the following:

- Whose voice is being forwarded in the drawing, presentations, tableau, and so on?
- Whose is not?
- Who stands to benefit from the artwork?
- Who does not?
- What message is the artist trying to convey?

Like artistic representations, a teacher can meet Common Core Anchor Standards for Speaking and Listening when teachers offer students opportunities to discuss and collaborate with one another, such as the following:

Connecting to Common Core State Standards

Comprehension and Collaboration

- Prepare for and participate effectively in a range of conversations and collaborations with diverse partners, building on others' ideas and expressing their own clearly and persuasively.

In discussions, teachers can encourage students to examine the visual representations for perspectives that may be dominant or silenced. Students will have the opportunity to analyze their own and others' art and performance. The purpose of analysis is not to condemn another's work, but rather to continue to examine history from a critical lens and revise our own historical beliefs based on new understandings.

Sarah's Classroom—Native People

We met Sarah, a third-grade bilingual teacher in Oakland, in Chapter 2. Sarah used the strategy of artifact analysis to open a five-lesson unit on the Ohlone people. In this lesson, Sarah paints a picture of the encounter between the Spanish colonizers and the Ohlone people from the perspective of the Ohlone people and then provides a space for students to apply content knowledge through performance.

To begin the lesson, Sarah asks students to remember what they have learned about the Ohlone people and their cultural and spiritual practices. She explains to them, "Today's objective will be to visualize and act out what the Spanish did when they arrived on Ohlone land and how the Ohlone acted." Sarah then draws her students' attention to key vocabulary words that will be used during the unit. Each word is accompanied by a definition and a picture. Students review the words by looking for similarities between Spanish and English and create sentences with their partners using the vocabulary words to demonstrate their understanding.

After students have completed their word work, Sarah reads to them the book *Encounter* (Yolen, 1996). Before beginning the story, she asks students to look at the title of the book and do a mini-picture analysis of the cover page to begin thinking about the content of the story. She provides them with a sentence frame, which is written on the front board: "I think this story is about _____ because _____."

Sarah reads the story to her students, asking critical questions throughout the reading, such as "Why might the indigenous people have trusted the Europeans? What do you think you would have done? What might the Taino boy have felt when nobody listened to him?"

After finishing the read-aloud, Sarah gives each student a paragraph describing what happened when the Spanish arrived. The students read the paragraph together using the method of "popcorn reading." In popcorn reading, a student reads a sentence or paragraph and then says "popcorn" and the name of another student in the class. The student whose name is called jumps in and starts to read where the previous student left off. The purpose of this activity is to keep students on track. Students can say "pass" if they do not want to read when called on.

Paragraph (Written by Sarah)

The Ohlone people lived peacefully in the area between San Francisco and Monterey for centuries before the Spanish colonizers came to what we now call California. When the Spanish arrived, the Ohlone were friendly and shared their food and culture with them. The Spanish wanted to convert the Ohlone to Christianity. They built missions and took some of them there to baptize them. They made the Ohlone work very hard for no pay and forced them to dress, eat, and speak like Spaniards. Most of the Ohlone did not want this, and many of them tried to run away, but if the Spanish found them, they would brutally beat them or kill them to scare other Ohlone so they would not try to run away. Because the Spanish brought many diseases that the Ohlone's bodies had never been around, many Ohlone died and the new babies did not live very long. The Ohlone population became smaller and smaller over time and that made it easier for the Spanish to control the land.

TABLE 4.3. Cause and Effect T-Chart

What the Spanish Did	How the Ohlone Reacted
• Spanish arrived.	• Ohlone were friendly, offered food, and shared culture.
• Spanish built missions and forced Ohlone to work and convert to Christianity.	• Ohlone were forced to move to missions, become Christian, and work without pay.
• Spanish beat and killed Ohlone who tried to run away to scare others.	• Some Ohlone tried to run away from the missions.
• Spanish brought diseases that were new to Ohlone.	• Many Ohlone died from diseases brought by Spanish.

After reading the text, Sarah and her students collaboratively create a cause and effect T-chart (see Table 4.3). Using the T-chart to guide discussion, Sarah then engages students in a group discussion around the following questions:

- What do you think the Ohlone thought when the Europeans did not share their things?
- Why do you think Europeans were able to force the Ohlone people to do things?
- Why did the Europeans want the Ohlone to become Christian?
- Why do you think some Ohlone ran away? Why do you think some Ohlone decided not to run away?
- What do you think the Europeans thought when the Ohlone shared their things with them?

After discussion, Sarah instructs her students to work in groups of four to act out one of the scenarios she provides about the encounter between the Spanish and Ohlone. She reminds students to consider what they learned from the paragraph, the book *Encounter* (Yolen, 1996), prior knowledge, and the T-chart.

Scenario 1: The Spanish arrive and meet the Ohlone people for the first time.
Scenario 2: The Spanish force Ohlone to become Christian and to work as slaves.
Scenario 3: Some Ohlone run away from the mission.
Scenario 4: Spanish bring diseases that are new to the Ohlone.

When each group is finished sharing their skit, Sarah brings the class together for a closing discussion. She ends the lesson by asking students to complete an exit slip with answers to the following questions before leaving the classroom:

- What did the Ohlone people do when they met the Spanish colonizers?
- What did the Spanish colonizers force the Ohlone to do?
- What happened to the Ohlone who tried to run away?
- Why did so many Ohlone people die after the Spanish arrived?

In this lesson, Sarah uses a variety of strategies to paint a picture of the encounter between the Natives and the Spanish colonizers. She builds students' background knowledge by reading aloud the picture book *Encounter* (Yolen, 1996) and engaging students in a collaborative reading of a text from the Ohlone perspective. By integrating social studies and language arts content, Sarah can meet the following ELA Common Core Standards for Reading: Literature, grade 3:

Connecting to Common Core State Standards

Key Ideas and Details

RL.3.1. Ask and answer questions to demonstrate understanding of text, referring explicitly to the text as the basis for the answers.

RL.3.2. Recount stories; determine the central message, lesson, or moral and explain how it is conveyed through key details in the text.

RL.3.3. Describe characters in a story and explain how their actions contribute to the sequence of the events.

Sarah could cover these standards in her lesson by asking students critical comprehension questions following the read-aloud of *Encounter* (Yolen, 1996) and the popcorn reading of her self-developed paragraph. Sarah could ask comprehension questions pertaining to key details of the text, including questions about the characters and their actions in the story.

Sarah provides many scaffolds and structures to help all the learners in her classroom access content knowledge. For example, she begins her lesson building on students' prior knowledge by asking students to recall what they learned in previous lessons. She asks students to make predictions about what the book *Encounter* (Yolen, 1996) might be about. She provides sentence frames for students to use as a support to structure their words and writing. In addition, she takes significant time to review key vocabulary before engaging in the lesson. As she provides multiple opportunities for students to collaborate, either in partners or in groups, she gives her students the chance to learn from one another. Last, Sarah uses exit cards as a means for quick assessment to determine what her students learned from the lesson and also another space for students to process and apply information.

In this lesson Sarah creates a direct link between two tenets, uncovering the past and exploring multiple perspectives (painting the picture) and synthesizing content knowledge through performance (application). She leans on performance as a platform for her students to synthesize the material they accessed through read-alouds, graphic organizers, and prior learning.

If Sarah were limited with time, she could translate her read-aloud and popcorn reading activity into her language arts period. As Sarah is already covering language arts Common Core Standards for Reading, she could justify how she was integrating social studies content in language arts. If Sarah did not have time to do the role play during language arts, she could make space for the activity during an alternate time period.

Sarah could also lean on her social studies textbook to build students' background knowledge of the Ohlone people. As students critically read the description of the Ohlone people in their textbooks, students could answer the following questions:

- What was told in the read-aloud and the paragraph that is not said in our textbooks? Why?
- Whose voice is heard? Whose is not?
- What might we add to our textbooks to include more of the Ohlone perspective?

In conclusion, art and performance play an important role in a social justice–oriented social studies classroom. They provide a space for students to process and apply content knowledge, while also allowing students to be imaginative and creative. Art and performance can be especially appealing to our English language learners, as our English language learners may be able to demonstrate their understanding of content through a medium that may be less restrictive than other avenues.

REWRITING THE NARRATIVE

The narrative presented in our social studies textbooks often limits the voices and perspectives of many members of our society. The often-biased version of history denies our children the opportunity to learn social studies from multiple perspectives. For many students, their ancestors' contributions, struggles, and resistance are invisible in traditional texts, resulting in students not getting to see how their ancestors' efforts made change in this world.

As a space for synthesis and application, students can rewrite a narrative so that it is inclusive of others' voices. Based on what students gather during lessons where the teacher has painted the picture, students can develop a story line either individually or collectively that forwards a narrative of a person or group that may be silenced in their textbooks. VanSledright (2002) explains:

> This process opens up a host of opportunities for children to learn about themselves. It enables them to see that we humans choose, create, and manipulate stories we convey about ourselves and the ways we use them to live our lives. This is empowering because it teaches students that they, too, can have a hand in the process. It provides a window and encourages children to club through, to participate in action. (p. 149)

Encouraging our students to reconceptualize history through a lens that is inclusive of all members of our society is an important piece of social justice–oriented social studies teaching. By rewriting history to include a silenced perspective, our students may see themselves as having an active and participatory role in their learning. The purpose of the book is to re-create social studies content from a perspective that may be silenced or limited in traditional social studies textbooks.

To begin, students gather in groups to discuss the historical event they have been studying and to determine whose perspective of the event they wish to share. For example, after studying the Louisiana Purchase, a group may decide to rewrite the narrative presented in their textbook from a Native American perspective. Once a perspective has been decided, students move through the stages of a Writers' Workshop: prewriting, drafting, revising, and editing. A group may allocate some members to do the writing, while others do the illustrations. In the revision phase, groups may analyze their books with critical reading questions such as the ones we discussed during the book review:

- What was the author's message or intent?
- How do you feel about the main character in the book? Can you relate to him or her?
- Who was the book written for?
- Whose perspective do we get to hear?
- Whose perspective do we not get to hear?
- Who may be missing from the story line?
- Is the story based on historical evidence?

In minilessons, we may teach and model for our students specific writing skills including:

- Constructing a story line
- Developing characters
- Choosing between fiction and nonfiction
- Creating sound historical interpretations

Students will need significant scaffolding and support through the writing process. Graphic organizers such as flow charts and webs may be especially helpful in the prewriting phase to help students organize their thoughts. Webs may also help students develop their characters if they are writing fictional books.

When students have moved through the entire Writers' Workshop process and completed their books, they can publish their books. Each group can take turns reading their stories to the class. Teachers can invite parents to the event as well. The purpose of the publishing and celebrating is to honor students' efforts and hard work.

In this activity, students write their interpretations of history and support their claims with evidence. Students may also have to gather information from multiple sources to support their analysis and reflection. Moreover, students develop and strengthen their work through the writing process of planning, revising, editing, and publishing. Because of the depth of this activity, a teacher could address the following Common Core Anchor Standards for Writing:

Connecting to Common Core State Standards

Production and Distribution of Writing

- Produce clear and coherent writing in which the development, organization, and style are appropriate to task, purpose, and audience.
- Develop and strengthen writing as needed by planning, revising, editing, rewriting, or trying a new approach.
- Use technology, including the Internet, to produce and publish writing and to interact and collaborate with others.

Research to Build and Present Knowledge

- Draw evidence from literary or informational texts to support analysis, reflection, and research.

By writing their own narrative of history, students can engage in an activity that challenges them to write and share their interpretations of history in light of what they have gathered, learned, and processed. Students can collaborate with one another and engage in healthy debates about what should or should not be included in their text. They can provide for others an interpretation of history that may not be visible in their textbooks so that their peers and future generations can learn from what they have learned, offering others a critical understanding of social studies from multiple perspectives.

CONCLUSION

After the teacher paints the picture of what really happened, students need time and space to create their own understandings of history. The purpose of application is for students to synthesize and process content information. To do this, we provide a space for students to grapple with what they know and what they have learned to piece together their own interpretations of history.

The examples offered in this chapter present ways to process social studies content through mediums less structured than writing and speaking. Art and performance may allow a safer space for students to translate their inner conceptions and ideas around history. Students are still engaging in academically rigorous curriculum, an important aspect of social justice teaching, but they are applying and processing their historical interpretations through a platform other than structured writing.

Even with limited time, teachers can use a graphic organizer as a space for students to synthesize and process information. Teachers can use a graphic organizer prior to having students write poems or engage in an activity. If a teacher does not have time to extend students' ideas into a poem, role play, tableau, or something else, a graphic organizer, in itself, serves as an important place for students to organize, process, and apply social studies content knowledge. Some examples of graphic organizers are T-charts, Venn diagrams, flow charts, and webs.

Most of the strategies described in this section create a product (e.g., poem, collage, book, and so on) from which teachers can gain valuable information to assess their students. Assessment is a tool for teachers to understand what students are learning based on evidence collected from their work. For example, if a teacher were to ask students to create a collage as a space to apply and process information, she could create a rubric to assess her students' learning. In the rubric, the teacher identifies criteria for grading. For example, in the collage some criteria might include these questions: (1) Is the representation historically sound? (2) Did the student draw from primary and secondary resources? The rubric and criteria students are assessed on are shared with students prior to creating their collages so they have a clear understanding of what is expected. Students could continue to return to the rubric while creating their collages to make sure they are meeting the criteria on which they will be assessed.

While learning social justice–oriented social studies curriculum, students are engaged in a complex process where they are given multiple interpretations of history they have to synthesize and understand. In application, students are working to synthesize, process, and apply what they have learned in order to develop their own historical interpretations.

REFLECTION EXERCISES

The following are reflection exercises to help extend these concepts into class-room practice:

1. Why do we need to allocate a specific space for our students to synthesize and process their historical interpretations? What kind of space do we need?
2. How might art and performance be a space for students to apply and process content knowledge? How might you integrate art and performance into your social studies unit?
3. Most of the strategies described above could be easily integrated into a language arts period. How might you meet language arts Common Core Standards using one of the strategies described above (e.g., dialogue poems)?
4. What scaffolds or support systems could you use to support your English language learners and special needs students in the strategies shared above?
5. Think about the students in your classroom. Choose five students. What strategy would benefit them most in their effort to synthesize and process information?
6. What graphic organizers could you use as a scaffold to help your students with a specific activity (e.g., dialogue poems—Venn diagrams)?

CHAPTER 5

Connecting the Past to the Present

ONCE STUDENTS HAVE developed their understandings of critical social studies content, the next step is to challenge students to make concrete connections between the past and the present so they can see the ways in which our past determines and influences our present and future. By pressing students to make connections, teachers offer them the opportunity to see history as dynamic and intrinsically linked to our world today.

Thus far, the main objective of lessons has been to create opportunities for students to think deeply about social studies content. Through strategies such as simulation, artifact analysis, and literature circles, students grapple with historical content from multiple perspectives. Knowledge is not acquired through an input-output model, but rather a dynamic process in which students create their own interpretations of history through the examination of evidence and artifacts.

In this chapter, we extend from a place of synthesis and application toward a space in which we are connecting the past to contemporary social issues. By working to make explicit connections between the past and present, we provide students with opportunities to see how our society systematically continues to benefit some, while hurting others. We examine how the struggles and resistance of our ancestors and allies and their fight for social justice may help us to learn how we can make change in our society today.

Listed in this chapter are strategies you can use to draw explicit connections with your students between the past and the present. As in previous chapters, I also discuss how you can connect social studies content to language arts, meet language arts Common Core Standards, and lean on mandated curricular materials to find space to integrate the strategies discussed in this chapter.

CONTEXTUALIZING THE PRESENT USING THE PAST

As the past is no longer, all we have with us are the artifacts that can help us recover bits and pieces of what went on before our time (VanSledright, 2002). We may glean diary entries, films, photographs, or texts for data that might help us learn and reconstruct the stories of those who lived in the past, including the voices who may be silenced in mainstream historical narratives. Our understandings of history may change and evolve as we gather more information, synthesize, and create new meanings. When studying history, we are in an endless process of revising and reconstructing our interpretations.

The importance of constructing parallels and connections between the past and the present is for students to be able to see, systemically, that entities such as racism and discrimination still exist today and are deeply influenced and connected to actions in the past. As our past ancestors and allies refused to remain compliant in the face of injustice, so resistance, social movements, and organization also continue today. Our students can learn from the many stories of action taken by everyday citizens to work toward a socially just society (Wade, 2007). As they expand their horizons to world current events, what they see will also be informed by this learning.

Showing history and its relevance to the present is an important piece of social justice teaching. If the past remains in the past, students may feel guilty or helpless in learning about the injustices of yesterday, and powerless in their ability to make change. Students may also feel little personal responsibility or compassion toward what happened in the past, believing history as not relevant or connected to their own lives. Yet, if students are offered opportunities to connect the past to the present, they may find parallels between the injustices of yesterday and today. Students may feel empowered when learning about those who fought for social change, and thus be inspired to find ways to make change in their own communities. As social justice educators, we work to highlight the continuum of social injustices yesterday and today and integrate the efforts of our ancestors and allies who fought endlessly, often risking their lives, for a more just world.

For instance, slavery is a topic often expected to be covered in both the fourth- and fifth-grade social studies curriculum. Through the general curriculum, students may learn about the history of slavery in the United States, including the Civil War and the conflict between the North and the South, the secession of the South, the eradication of slavery in 1865 by the 13th Amendment, and the reconstruction era. Students may also learn through textbooks the courageous efforts of abolitionists such as Frederick Douglass, Nat Turner, William Lloyd Garrison, and Harriet Tubman.

After students have had enough time to critically examine and process content, a teacher could extend the discussion into the present by pressing to explore the implications of slavery today. By connecting the past to the present, slavery is depicted as not "something" that happened long ago, but an institution whose consequences continue to affect us deeply. Questions like the ones below may encourage students to make concrete connections between the past and the present:

- How is racism connected to slavery? How does our nation still struggle with the ramifications of slavery today?

- How can we learn from the abolitionists who fought to make change and eradicate slavery? What can we take away from these models to help us in our efforts today?
- Where else in the world does slavery exist today (e.g., Sudan)? What efforts could we take to help stop slavery?

Students could examine the questions in a whole-group discussion or the questions could become research projects that students could explore with small, collaborative groups. Through classroom discussion, a teacher could meet the following Common Core Anchor Standards for Speaking and Listening:

Connecting to Common Core State Standards

Comprehension and Collaboration

- Prepare for and participate effectively in a range of conversations and collaborations with diverse partners, building on others' ideas and expressing their own clearly and persuasively.

ALLOWING STUDENTS TO MAKE THE CONNECTION

As teachers facilitate discussion, students learn to build on others' ideas and express their own beliefs around how the past may work to inform and influence the present. Teachers can challenge students to make past-to-present connections during or after studying any historical event. For example, after studying the Indian Removal Act of 1830, a teacher may ask students to think about a contemporary issue that resembles what happened to Native Americans during the Indian Removal Act. The Indian Removal Act of 1830 forced many Native Americans to sign treaties that removed them from the lands they had lived in for thousands of years. During discussion, a teacher may introduce the idea of gentrification, as this may be affecting many of her students' families in the classroom. *Gentrification* is where wealthy people acquire and take over low-income neighborhoods. Families are "bought out" and forced to relocate to different neighborhoods that are more affordable. To make the connection between the past and present explicit, a teacher might ask her students questions like these:

- How is the Indian Removal Act of 1830 similar to gentrification? How is it different?
- Who was hurt in the Indian Removal Act? Who might be hurt through the process of gentrification?
- How did the Native Americans resist the Indian Removal Act?

TABLE 5.1. Connecting the Past to the Present

Past	Present
Encounter between Natives and Christopher Columbus (1492)	Gentrification
Mexican-American War (1846–1848)	Immigration laws, rights of undocumented workers
Great Depression (1929–1940)	Current economic recession
Civil Rights Movement (1955–1968)	Occupy Movement
Japanese Internment Camps (1942)	Anti-Muslim sentiment after 9/11

- What are people doing today to resist the gentrification of their neighborhoods?

Teachers can enrich their social studies curriculum whenever they can connect historical events to contemporary issues in the present. Other examples of connecting the past to the present are shown in Table 5.1.

As students critically think about past-to-present connections, we can remind them about how our ancestors and allies worked to make change in their communities. By learning how others worked toward change, students may learn how to organize and access the necessary tools and resources they need to take action. Students may consider questions such as: Who was involved in the action? What did they do? How were their actions successful? What resources did they need? Did they engage allies and if so, how? How was their message forwarded?

One way to do this is to have students list the acts of resistance they learned about when studying a particular historical event. Table 5.2 depicts an organizer to help students work through their thoughts. When filling out a graphic organizer such as this, students can peruse their textbook and other resource materials (e.g., Internet, encyclopedia, books) to help them gain more information.

Once students have compiled their lists, they may find similarities and commonalities between others' struggles and their struggles today. They may also connect emotionally to some of the suffering and hardships others faced and the pain they and their families face today. We can encourage our students to make emotional connections to past experiences by asking them questions such as: How does it feel to be discriminated against? How did our ancestors and allies feel? How do we feel when we are treated badly? People were intolerant toward each other in the past; how can we stand up for one another and build solidarity and alliance? How can we intervene and assist others when we see someone being discriminated against? How can we be an ally to them?

In connecting the past and the present, we are working intentionally to help students see how our society has continuously worked to benefit some

TABLE 5.2. Acts of Resistance Organizer

Act of Resistance	Description	Element
Greensboro, N.C. Sit-in (1960)	Four Black students from North Carolina's Agricultural and Technical School sat in peaceful protest because a waitress refused to serve them coffee at a Whites-only counter. This sparked the sit-in protest movement.	Sit-in
Freedom Riders (1961)	In an attempt to desegregate public facilities, freedom riders rode interstate busses to protest racial segregation in restaurants and waiting rooms in terminals serving buses that crossed state lines.	Sit-in
La Causa (1962)	Cesar Chavez organized a migrant farmworkers' strike and a 250-mile march as an effort to bring improvements in working conditions and pay for Hispanic farmworkers.	Strike and March
Selma-to-Montgomery Freedom March (1965)	Martin Luther King led this voting rights march in Alabama to demand equal voting rights for all Americans, regardless of race.	March

and hurt others. We are also looking to the past to find role models and inspiration to help us understand how we can make change in our schools, communities, and world today. It is our past that can help us picture a better future, to find hope and promise that we can live in a more just world. Linking the past to the present creates a particular path for students to see themselves in history and their possibility as agents for change.

DRAWING EXPLICIT CONNECTIONS

When connecting the past to the present, teachers can create connections between historical events and contemporary social issues. For example, when studying the Mexican-American War of 1846–1848 (as described in Chapter 3), a teacher may leverage strategies discussed in prior chapters such as artifact analysis, book review, and role play to help illustrate the war from the perspective of both the Mexicans and White Americans. After students have had the opportunity to process and apply content knowledge either through writing, drawing, or speaking, we can provide a space for them to make explicit connections between the past and the present.

When studying the Mexican-American War, a teacher could make direct links to the present by asking questions such as the following:

- During the Mexican-American War, the United States took control of half a million square miles of Mexican territory. Mexicans inside the United States were supposed to be guaranteed the same rights as citizens of the United States, yet were not. How do the consequences of the war continue to affect Mexicans living in America today?

- What did we learn about the Mexican-American War and the injustices Mexicans faced that may be directly linked to the present? How might public policies have served to hurt many Mexican Americans in the past and the present including Proposition 227 (1998), which served to dismantle bilingual education in most of California, or Arizona SB 1070 (2010), an anti-illegal immigration measure designed to require law enforcers to determine individuals' immigration status at will?
- What are the consequences of war? What did we learn about the Mexican-American War and the lives that were hurt that might be similar or different to the war in Afghanistan today?

In each sense, a teacher is intentionally creating a past-to-present link for his or her students, and then engaging students in a critical conversation and analysis around the historical event and a contemporary social issue. By connecting the past to the present, learning becomes more relevant and engaging to students. History is not just about the past, but deeply connected to our lives today.

Caroline's Classroom—Internment

We met Caroline, a fifth-grade teacher in San Francisco, in Chapter 3. She designed a unit plan for students to critically examine the meaning of the U.S. Constitution. In this section we see how Caroline extends from the past (three lessons examining the U.S. Constitution) into the present.

With her students seated on the floor in front of her, Caroline begins this lesson by saying:

Yesterday we discussed what would happen if you did not agree with certain laws. We learned that by taking action, we can make unfair rules unconstitutional such as segregation. Today, we will continue to explore how the words in our United States Constitution are just as important today as when it was written over 200 years ago. We will learn about a tragic time in our recent history—a time period in which my grandparents were living—in which a group of Americans lost their Constitutional rights based solely on their race and ancestry.

After sharing the objective, Caroline asks students, "What rights do you feel you deserve as citizens?" Next, Caroline shows students a music video (pulled from YouTube) that shows pictures of Japanese Americans losing their houses and having to relocate after the attack on Pearl Harbor in 1941. She asks students to look closely at the pictures and begin to think about what is happening, where the people are being sent, and why. After they watch the video, she asks students to think and respond to the following questions:

- Two thirds of those forced into relocation centers were American citizens. Why were they taken away?
- How do you feel about children being taken away?
- Why was fear and racial prejudice so strong at this time?

Caroline facilitates discussion around these guiding questions, and then asks students to spend time reviewing a Smithsonian Institution website entitled *A More Perfect Union: Japanese Americans & the U.S. Constitution* (http:/americanhistory.si.edu/perfectunion/experience/index.html).

Through the website Caroline hopes students will gain more content knowledge of the causes and effects of Executive Order 9066 (1942), the order which forced all Americans of Japanese descent into internment camps. While students explore the website they write about: (1) two quotes they found interesting; (2) one audio clip they found interesting and why; and (3) something interesting they discussed with their partner.

Caroline gathers her students back to the floor to continue the lesson. She asks her students, "Do you think this could happen today? If so, to what group of people?" She then asks students to close their eyes and imagine this scenario:

Three months after the September 11th attack on the Twin Towers in 2001, President Bush signs an Executive Order that requires all Muslim Americans to relocate for the sake of national security. This is agreed on by Congress without a dissenting vote.

After sharing that hypothetical scenario, Caroline asks students to write a letter from the point of view of a Muslim American who is facing internment. Students may write to whomever they want (friends, family, President, or others), but must include some aspect of the relocation process: removal, packing, discrimination, internment, or living situations. Students must also include a paragraph that describes how the legislation is unfair and why they want to try to make this enactment unconstitutional.

After students complete their letters, Caroline brings the lesson to a close by asking her students the following questions:

- Even though we did not read specific accounts of Muslim American perspectives, what ideas did you use to write your letter?

- What common themes do you notice?
- Why is it important to connect the past to the present?
- How does the U.S. Constitution affect us today?
- What can you do if you feel something is unconstitutional?

In this lesson, Caroline makes explicit connections between the past and the present for her students. After painting a picture of the U.S. Constitution through discussions, analytical readings, and so forth, Caroline extends to the present to connect the idea of Constitutional rights to recent historical decisions such as the effects of Executive Order 9066. Although a similar order was not issued at the time of 9/11, Caroline has students imagine the order being issued during the time of 9/11. As anti-Muslim sentiments after 9/11 paralleled anti-Japanese sentiments following the attack on Pearl Harbor, the connection allows students to see patterns of discrimination and injustice throughout our history. Students may question ideals surrounding justice and wonder how the U.S. Constitution can serve to protect some and not others.

Caroline uses many strategies to make learning accessible to all students in the classroom. She clearly states the objective of her lesson and also reviews students' prior learning around the subject matter. She uses many visuals, such as graphic organizers, video clips, and modeling. Students have several opportunities to think-pair-share and work in small groups. Caroline also has students write informally: (1) notes during the website review and (2) a letter from the perspective of a Muslim American. In each case, both writing assignments provide Caroline with an assessment tool for evaluating her students' learning.

Particularly important to note is Caroline's way of presenting social studies content from a capacity perspective. Although Japanese and Muslim Americans were forced to deal with internment, hate crimes, and extreme prejudice, she portrays their roles in history as dynamic, resistant, and active. For example, the website that Caroline asks her students to explore about Japanese Americans after the attack on Pearl Harbor allows students to see how Japanese Americans resisted relocation and remained resilient even through the horrors of their internment. Secondly, Caroline asks her students to write a letter from a Muslim American perspective with a mandatory paragraph that describes how students will make the enactment unconstitutional. The narratives of members of our society who have been discriminated against and unfairly treated are provided in a capacity where they are viewed as empowered, strong, and resilient.

Caroline devotes an entire class period to the fourth tenet of the framework, connecting the past to the present. If Caroline had to use her mandated curriculum and was limited with time, she could have students critically examine their textbook's portrayal of 9/11 to examine what major ideas emerged from the excerpt and who is celebrated and who is silenced. Caroline could then condense this lesson into a few critical questions which could evoke conversation that connects the past to the present.

Caroline could also easily integrate this lesson into her language arts period. As the beginning of the lesson is particularly oriented toward social studies, Caroline could teach the first half of the lesson during her social studies period, which is primarily focused on eliciting students' prior knowledge and building background. Caroline could then use her language arts period toward the letter-writing activity. In a minilesson Caroline could model for her students using chart paper or the overhead how to write an informal and formal letter. She could share a letter she wrote from the perspective of a Muslim American to the class. After modeling the activity, Caroline could then have students work on their letters through a writing process that allows them to prewrite, draft, revise, edit, and publish their writing. She could provide graphic organizers and sentence frames to support her English language learners. She could pull small groups while others are working independently to provide extra support.

By explicitly teaching letter writing to her students, Caroline could meet the following ELA Common Core Standards for Writing, grade 5:

Connecting to Common Core State Standards
Text Types and Purposes
W.5.3. Write narratives to develop real or imagined experiences or events using effective technique, descriptive details, and clear event sequences.

Through minilessons, Caroline could teach her students narrative techniques such as dialogue and description and/or ways in which to use sensory details to express events and experiences concretely.

The intention of connecting the past to the present is for students to explicitly see how the injustices of today are deeply contextualized into the fabric of today's society. If limited with time, asking even one question to students at least allows students to see how parallels exist between the past and the present, including themes around injustice and resistance.

Jen's Classroom—The Transcontinental Railroad

Jen is a fourth-grade teacher in San Francisco, California. She designed a curriculum unit that studies the building of the Transcontinental Railroad from the Chinese perspective. In prior lessons Jen worked intentionally to develop students' critical lenses. She inspired wonder and painted the picture for her students of the historical event from Chinese perspectives through textbook readings, picture walk of illustrations and photos from the building of the Transcontinental Railroad period, and read-alouds (e.g., *Tales from*

Gold Mountain (Yee & Ng, 1989/2011), *Coolies* (Yin, 2003). She provided a space for application in a letter activity which asked students to draw on content knowledge to write a letter from the perspective of a Chinese railroad worker. In this lesson Jen works to connect past issues of injustice to current issues of exploitation.

Jen begins the lesson reminding students of the treatment of the Chinese workers during the building of the Transcontinental Railroad. She refers back to the webs they developed collaboratively with their groups that detailed the emotional hardships and struggles, as well as the successes and contributions, of the Chinese during the building of the Transcontinental Railroad. After reviewing the vocabulary, Jen asks her students, "Are workers treated this poorly today?"

Once students have shared their thoughts, Jen asks students to look at the Nike logo on the front board. Jen says, "Put your thumbs up if you recognize this logo." Jen then shows her students a picture of a pair of $150 Nike shoes and a picture of the Nike CEO with his salary written underneath the picture ($7.6 million). She then shows students a picture of a Nike sweatshop in South Korea with the salary of a sweatshop worker written underneath ($26 a month). After this, Jen shows students pictures of the Disney, Old Navy, Gap, and Levi's logos and writes how much each company profits a year.

Jen then shows students pictures of sweatshops and discusses the working conditions in sweatshops and on farms, including the long hours for little pay and descriptions of the dangerous conditions. She explains the words *poverty, logo, CEO, wage, minimum wage, living wage,* and *pesticides* to her students and adds the words to the word wall.

She then looks at the average rent for a one-bedroom apartment in San Francisco: $1,400 a month. She asks students to figure out how much it would cost to rent an apartment for a year (12 x $1,400). Once students have done the math, she asks, "How does a farmworker pay $16,800 a year for an apartment when he or she only makes $7,500 a year? How do they pay for rent, food, bills, clothing, medical bills, and so on?" Jen also explains that women make on average 77 cents for every dollar that a man makes for doing the same job. Jen then gives her students the following questions to discuss in groups:

- Do men work harder than women?
- Do the CEOs of Nike or Dole work harder than the farmworkers or garment workers?
- Did the boss on the railroads work harder than the Chinese workers?
- How much money did the Big Four make?
- How much money did the Chinese workers make?

After students have had the opportunity to discuss the questions in groups, Jen brings her students back together to discuss the questions as a whole group. She reminds students that despite the immense contributions of the Chinese to the building of the Transcontinental Railroad, the workers could not afford to ride the trains. This remains the same today. It would be too costly for a sweatshop worker to buy the clothes he or she makes, and for a farmworker to buy produce from Trader Joe's or Whole Foods grown on his farm.

As closure to the lesson, Jen asks students to write about the treatment of the Chinese workers during the building of the Transcontinental Railroad and the treatment of workers today. Have things changed? Why or why not? How do you feel about this?

Jen made an explicit connection for her students between the unfair working conditions of the past to the present. In this way students can connect past issues of injustice to current issues of exploitation and discrimination in today's world. Through discussion around the past and the present, Jen could meet the following ELA Common Core Standards for Speaking and Listening, grade 4:

Connecting to Common Core State Standards

Comprehension and Collaboration

SL.4.1. Engage effectively in a range of collaborative discussions (one-on-one, in groups, and teacher-led) with diverse partners on grade 4 topics and texts, building on others' ideas and expressing their own clearly.

By connecting the past and the present, students may be better able to see how systemically our society has worked to benefit some and not others. When students get opportunities to see injustice and efforts toward change, students may be driven to try to make change in their communities and world. In her next lesson, facilitating action, Jen has students take action by creating a schoolwide flyer encouraging students and their families to support immigrant workers' rights.

Like Caroline, Jen dedicates an entire period to the fourth tenet of this framework, painting the picture. If limited with time, Jen could frontload the vocabulary during language arts and teach the remainder of the lesson during the social studies period. She could also give her students more background knowledge around sweatshops and low wages by finding articles and read-alouds that she could share with them during language arts. This would give Jen more time to dedicate toward social studies and also integrate content across two subject areas, providing students with multiple reinforcement of concepts throughout the day.

John's Classroom—The Great Depression and the Recession

We met John while learning strategies to help us paint the picture in Chapter 3. John is a fifth-grade teacher in San Francisco. John taught students about the Great Depression through strategies such as simulation, role play, graphic organizers, and read-alouds to help students see multiple perspectives surrounding the Great Depression. As a space for application, John had students pretend to be journalists writing newspaper articles about the photographs they studied in prior lessons.

In this lesson, John has students compare and contrast the Great Depression with our current recession by connecting the struggles of the past to the present in open group discussion. The lesson begins with John having students gather together on the rug for discussion. On the projector is a video review of the movie *The Grapes of Wrath*, comparing the Great Depression to our modern recession (Johnson, 2008). After watching the film, John shares the story of his grandmother who migrated from Oklahoma to California. Her story is like the one told in *The Grapes of Wrath*. Like many farmers, John's grandparents were indebted to the banks because they could not afford to pay. For that reason, his grandparents lost their farm to the banks and sold all of their possessions to move to California in hope of a better life. John reminds his students, "Today, like the past, many people are losing their homes to banks because they cannot make their mortgage payments."

John explains to students, "Some people think the economic situation of today is similar to the economic situation leading up to the Great Depression. What are some of the recent issues with the economy?" After students list issues such as buying on credit, lack of jobs, foreclosures, bankruptcy, homelessness, and stock market crash, John asks students to list some of the issues with the economy preceding the Great Depression. Once both lists are created, students get into groups of four or five to create Venn diagrams. Once students have completed their Venn diagrams, John engages his students in discussion by asking, "What parallels do you see between the Great Depression and our current economic recession?"

To connect the past to the present, John makes an explicit connection between the Great Depression and our current recession. John provides students with a video clip and a graphic organizer to help his students compare and contrast similarities and differences between the two economic situations. Some students may need more time to gain background knowledge about the current recession. John could have students read and discuss newspaper articles about the current recession in literature circles. Through this activity, John could meet the following ELA Common Core Standards for Reading: Informational Text, grade 5 on page 112.

> **Connecting to Common Core State Standards**
>
> *Key Ideas and Details*
>
> RI.5.2. Determine two or more main ideas of a text and explain how they are supported by key details; summarize the text.
>
> *Craft and Structure*
>
> RI.5.6. Analyze multiple accounts of the same event or topic, noting important similarities and differences in the point of view they represent.

By having students engage in a critical reading of a newspaper article around the current recession, John can deepen students' background knowledge and meet language arts Common Core Standards. He can encourage students to draw main ideas from the text and analyze their group's article against information presented in another group. Graphic organizers may be particularly useful in comparing and contrasting information and perspectives presented in articles, as students can share information openly and easily.

As many of John's students and their families may be suffering from the consequences of the recession directly, John could have students share or write about how they, their families, and/or friends have struggled through this difficult economic time. For example, maybe a student's parent was laid off from work and is having difficulty finding a job; or perhaps a family could not make their mortgage payments and lost their home to foreclosure. By directly connecting to students' lived experiences, students may better connect with the subject matter.

Through this lesson, John created an important space for students to connect the past to the present. By comparing and contrasting two economic situations, students were able to draw parallels between the Great Depression and our current recession. In his next lesson, John could have students think about what we can do to improve our economic condition.

PROVIDING OPPORTUNITIES FOR STUDENTS TO MAKE CONNECTIONS

In providing students with the opportunity to make their own connections, they are offered the chance to find a past-to-present connection that is applicable and relevant to their own lives. As we provide our students with opportunities to choose, we also learn from our students more about their lives and the social issues affecting them on a daily basis. As Ayers (2001) explains, "if understanding students is a central goal, afford children multiple opportunities to choose, to initiate, to create during some part of classroom life" (p. 38). Choice offers students the opportunity to construct connections meaningful and relevant to them and a chance for us, as teachers, to learn more about our students. For example, a student may connect a study on Native American relocation to the gentrification of his neighborhood. A student may have had to move or lose her home due to the increase in rent. Or a student may connect a study of the Chinese Exclusion Act to the lack of workers' rights for migrant farmworkers. Students may see their parents or themselves dealing with unfair working conditions and low wages so that they cannot support their families.

Students can brainstorm connections and then choose one part to discuss in detail. Graphic organizers, such as a Venn diagram or T-chart, may be helpful to compare and contrast the past and the present. Students can also list key figures and groups in the past and the present who have worked and are working to make change. Once students have completed their graphic organizers, they can share their past-to-present connections with the rest of the class. As groups share, students can look for points of intersection between the past and the present and ways in which our society has historically worked to benefit some and not others.

Anna's Classroom—Power and Unequal Distribution of Resources

Anna is a fourth-grade teacher in San Francisco, California. In a unit on the California missions, Anna designed lessons for students to examine pre-Columbian daily life, including the structure of pre-Columbian settlements, food/cooking, culture, beliefs, and religion. To inspire wonder and paint the picture, Anna elicited strategies such as KWLQ charts, textbook readings, simulations, and guest speakers. For application, Anna asked her students to write a journal entry as if they were native people going through change. Students needed to describe feelings, emotions, and concerns. In this lesson, students connect past struggles of injustice to contemporary social issues of today.

To begin, Anna has a colleague act as the teacher when her students return from lunch. In the classroom, everything has been removed from the desks and placed into plastic bags in a pile at the back of the room. Backpacks, hats, jackets, and any other possessions are also placed in plastic bags and moved to the back of the classroom.

When students enter the room, a piece of cloth with a hole at the center is given to them. Students are expected to wear the cloth over their clothing. The hole in the center is for their head. Students are also given a name tag, with their "new" name. If students speak or protest, their names are written on the board. The students with names on the board will be kept after school as a punishment to their resistance.

After a few minutes, Anna reappears in her classroom to explain that the activity was a simulation. She introduces her colleague, who has been acting as their teacher. She explains to students that this simulation was designed for students to better understand how the routines, practices, and lives of Native Americans were changed while living on Spanish settlements. She asks students, "Who was in control? What ways did you feel powerful? In what ways did you feel powerless?" She continues the conversation asking students to explain what made certain people powerful in that simulation, as well as to think about who was given power in the missions.

As students finish their discussion, Anna connects the past to the present by asking her students to think about the division of power in today's society. Who has power? Who does not have power? What determines whether you have power or not? How could this change? Students respond to her questions in an open discussion, facilitated by their teacher. Anna ends the lesson reviewing some of the points made by her students.

In this lesson, Anna uses simulation for her students to experience the coercive acts of missionaries, including labor demands, forced religious practices, and forced separation of children from families. She engages students in a creative simulation that allows them to experience, on an emotional level, what it must have been like for the Natives to have their possessions, home, and family taken away from them.

Anna could also provide opportunities for her students to see Native resistance. For example, although Native Americans were forced to convert to Christianity, many Natives continued to worship their old deities, as well as conduct native dances and rituals in secret (Castillo, 2011). According to Castillo (2011), a frequent form of resistance was fugitivism. Many Native Americans fled the missions and/or revolted against mission control. By pointing out how others fought and resisted injustice, we may inspire and empower our students to fight for change in the same way.

In connecting the past to the present, Anna allows her students a space to discuss issues surrounding the unequal distribution of power and resources today. She leaves the conversation open, so that students can construct connections of how they see power divided among the world and why. She also challenges students to think about how the unequal distribution of power might be mediated to make change. This creates a nice transition into her next lesson, facilitating change.

By engaging students in critical discussions surrounding past-to-present connections, Anna can meet ELA Common Core Standards for Speaking and Listening, grade 4 on the next page.

Through discussion, Anna can offer her students opportunities to draw on their prior knowledge and learning to explore new ideas in light of what they have learned. Anna can also elicit critical questions that challenge students to think analytically and express their ideas and beliefs.

Connecting to Common Core State Standards
Comprehension and Collaboration
SL.4.1. Engage effectively in a range of collaborative discussions (one-on-one, in groups, and teacher-led) with diverse partners on grade 4 topics and texts, building on others' ideas and expressing their own clearly.

Making It Work for You

Anna focuses on the simulation for most of her lesson and connects the past to the present only to close the lesson. Unlike Jen, who focused her entire lesson toward connecting the past to the present, Anna spent less than a third of her lesson toward this tenet of the framework. When working with the framework presented in this book, different amounts of time might be designated for different tenets. The tenets of the framework may also be applied in a different order. For example, in Anna's unit, she moves from inspiring wonder to painting the picture, to connecting the past to the present, to application, and then ends with facilitating change.

Other teachers' lessons we have looked at follow the framework presented in this book more closely. When deciding how to structure a unit or lesson plan, choose elements of the framework and strategies you think will work most appropriately for the lesson you are enacting in your classroom. You may choose bits and pieces from the strategies and tenets presented in this book, or use the framework exactly to construct a unit which begins with inspiring wonder and ends with facilitating change.

CONCLUSION

In this chapter we extend from our critical analysis of the past to make concrete connections to the present so that our students begin to draw parallels between what once was and what is becoming. As we make explicit connections between the past and the present, we work to see patterns throughout our history that have served to benefit some while hurting others. We also see the work of our ancestors and allies who have struggled and resisted to make change for the world we live in now. By learning how others fought for us and with us, we may see ourselves as both a "product of history and a potential agent for social change" (Hursh & Ross, 2000, p. 11). We can learn from others to see the capacity in ourselves to fight for our rights and the rights of others.

In this chapter I presented two strategies, drawing explicit connections and providing opportunities for students to make their own connections. In drawing explicit connections, a teacher creates an intentional link between the past and the present for students to explore. Teachers may build background for students around the contemporary issue and then use discussion, writing, or projects as a space for students to critically examine the connection between the past historical event they just studied and a contemporary issue affecting their community or society at large. In the second strategy, students create their own connections. Teachers may challenge their students to make connections between the past and the present by asking questions such as, "How is this historical event connected to what is happening today?" In using guiding questions, students have the choice and opportunity to construct connections to the present that may be directly affecting their everyday lives. When giving students the opportunity to choose, they may be able to create connections that personally affect them. In the end, both strategies offer students the opportunity to see the past as intrinsically linked to the present.

In thinking of ways to integrate social studies content into language arts, you could use the reading comprehension strategy of making connections as a way to bridge social studies and language arts content. In teaching students to make text-to-world connections, a teacher can simultaneously challenge students to make past-to-present connections. In this way, a teacher is able to meet language arts Common Core Standards for Speaking and Listening by engaging students in in-depth discussion and teaching social studies for social justice.

Most of the lessons presented in this chapter dedicated an entire period to this lesson. However, if limited with time, you could use one or two discussion questions as a way for students to connect the past to the present. For example, when studying the American Revolution, you could ask your students, "What is happening in the present that may simulate, parallel, or continue from the American Revolution?" In this way, you are still offering your students the opportunity to see the past as intrinsically linked to the present. By drawing connections between the past and the present, students are better engaged with the subject matter, as the connection to contemporary issues may be more relevant to our students' lives today.

Once students have had the opportunity to look analytically at a historical event from multiple perspectives, process and construct an understanding of what may have happened during the historical event and then engage in discussions surrounding the past and the present, the next step would be to funnel students' feelings and emotions that are tied to present-day social issues into a project around social change. Such a discussion and plan for social change is the way to conclude a social justice–oriented social studies unit.

REFLECTION EXERCISES

The following are reflection exercises to help extend these concepts into class-room practice:

1. What are ways in which we can connect the past to the present? Why is it important to make connections between the past and the present?
2. How might a teacher using the reading comprehension strategy of making connections find a space during language arts to enact strategies listed in this section?
3. Review your grade-level content standards and choose one historical event. How might you connect this event to a contemporary social issue?
4. How can linking the past to the present encourage students to be social change agents?
5. What are ways you could build background around contemporary social issues so that students can draw links between the past and the present?

CHAPTER 6

Facilitating Change

I N FACILITATING CHANGE, we transition from connecting the past to the present to investigating ways we can work to make change in our schools and communities. By facilitating change in the classroom, we empower our students to collaborate, organize, and take action and to reaffirm their role in shaping the world today.

In this chapter, students build off what they have learned about struggle, resistance, and social change during their social studies unit to examine and implement a social action project particular to their school and/or community. Students draw from their understandings of past resistance to determine how to take action, organize, and access the necessary resources and information. As students work collaboratively on a social action project, they find allies in the school and community to join them in their fight for social change. Through collaboration and action, students may better see themselves as active, participating, and influential members of society.

REAFFIRMING THE ROLE OF YOUTH

Facilitating action requires us to have an understanding of concepts such as fairness, equity, and discrimination. When students understand the roots of injustice and are given opportunities to examine the inequities prevalent within their school, community, and world, they may be inspired to desire and hope for change. In social justice–oriented social studies lessons, we examine and raise questions about the ways in which our society has systematically served to benefit some and hurt others.

As we ask our children to critique the world and question the status quo, we must also offer students the chance to identify and work on social problems. If we fail to empower our students to organize, collaborate, and act, critically questioning and examining the status quo may only serve to leave our students with feelings of guilt, anger, and helplessness. Students may see no possibility for change and feel powerless in their efforts to take action for what they believe in.

A student named Marisol gave this example:

For students of color, when curriculum is only about analyzing discrimination and oppression and not about allowing students to see the strength that they hold with their histories or what one can do to make change, the curriculum in this regard reinforces and reaffirms for students of color that they are on the outside and they need help.

By transitioning to discussions around social action, students may find hope and inspiration in the possibility of change. Students need to see and learn from those in the past who resisted, especially those who may look like them. By seeing people from all cultures who acted to make a difference, students may feel connected to and inspired by how their ancestors and allies sacrificed to make a better world for us (Bigelow, Harvey, and Karp, 2004). As students learn from those in the past who resisted, they may recognize a strength in themselves to make change.

Once students have a critical understanding of the past and an understanding of how people struggled and resisted, we can help our students recognize how to make change in the present. Students can learn from the organizing efforts of those who resisted, using their efforts as a model to understand how to engage like-minded allies and access necessary resources. As Loewen (2007) notes, "helping students understand what happened in the past empowers them to use history as a weapon to argue for better policies in the present" (p. 17). In this way students can learn from those who struggled and resisted to understand how they can make a difference today. Students can use models of organizing efforts in the past to plan their steps of action in the present. Students may consider questions such as: Who was involved in the action? What did they do? Were their actions successful? What would I change or do differently? What resources did they need? Did they engage allies and if so, how? How was their message forwarded? In this way, students can use the past as an important resource and model of how to make change in the present.

By creating a space for our students to see themselves as change makers and empowering them to take action in their schools and communities, we reaffirm the idea that we can all be change makers. As teachers committed to social justice, we have the capability and influence to engender a desire in students to transform inequalities and "become healers and changers of the world" (Adams, Bell, & Griffin, 1997, p. xiv). It is the acts of ordinary people like us who take small steps toward big change. The actions of students can work to provide awareness to others of what is unjust and inspire others to change what may be unfair or unjust. As students work toward change, they determine causes they wish to fight for and collaborate with one other to implement their social action project.

Students can write letters to city council members or their principal, create a petition, plan a fund-raiser, or create a poster sharing information about

TABLE 6.1. Social Action Project Planning

Stage	Reflective Questions
Examining the social issue	• If so many people know about this problem, why do you think it still exists? • Who might be benefiting from the situation as it currently exists? • What values might be motivating them? What do they want or need? • Has anyone tried to block solutions? How? What happened? • What's already being done? • What still needs to be done?
Designing the project	• What are your goals for the project? • Who will be involved in the project? • Who will the project help/support? • Why did you choose this project? • What information do you need? What will you need to learn? • What are your challenges? What will you need to think about? • How will you connect with others who may not think the same way?
Finding resources	• What resources will you need (writers, designers, speakers, thinkers, coaches, artists, advocates, devil's advocates)? • Who are your allies? Who may want to help you (like-minded individuals)?
Learning from the past	• What models of resistance did you learn from this unit that may help you organize for your social action project? What were their actions? What were they fighting for? How did they make change?

Note. Adapted from L. Schmidt, *Social Studies That Sticks: How to Bring Content and Concepts to Life* (Portsmouth, NH: Heinemann, 2007).

what they wish to change and why it is harmful in its current condition. Teachers can remind students that sometimes it is the small steps that can inspire big change.

Designing and implementing a social project can be a complex and difficult task for both children and adults. Therefore, it is essential that we provide structures to help our students plan how they will access necessary resources and information. Table 6.1 lists some important questions for students to consider before beginning their project. The questions will help students decide how to organize their social action project.

Using the questions as a guide, students can work in groups to understand the social issue they wish to investigate, the barriers they perceive might exist to changing the problem, and how they will implement their social action project. Graphic organizers, such as flow charts, webs, or T-charts may be helpful tools for students to organize their information. Assigning students one group of questions at a time allows them to focus on answering a few questions, instead of many questions at once.

ALIGNING SOCIAL JUSTICE GOALS

Although your students may be learning more about critical and higher order thinking through a social action project than a text-driven lesson, you will most likely still need to explain to your administration how your students' participation in social action projects is addressing standards. When familiarizing yourself with the Common Core Standards for language arts, you will find that many of the standards are deeply aligned with the critical and higher order thinking skills students need to engage in social action projects. For example, a class may choose to write a formal letter to the district addressing school lunches for their social action project. In the letter the students detail: (1) the consequences of eating an unhealthy lunch daily; (2) the obesity rates in children; (3) a cost comparison of an unhealthy lunch to a healthy lunch; and (4) the benefits of eating a healthy lunch.

During Writers' Workshop, the teacher models for her students how to write a formal letter. She includes minilessons each day designed to help students create a clear and organized formal letter. For example, she models for students how to support arguments with evidence from information texts. To construct their letter, students continue through a writing process which includes prewriting, revising, editing, drafting, and typing the final draft of the letter. Once students have completed their letter, the teacher mails the letter to the district. The social action project could cover the following Common Core Anchor Standards for Writing (if each standard was explicitly taught in minilessons during Writers Workshop) listed on page 122.

As part of the social action project, students might also decide to present their argument at a school district meeting. In a 5-minute speech using PowerPoint slides, a group of students explains to school administration, board members, parents, and other member committees the details of their letter and argument for why unhealthy lunches should be replaced with healthy lunches. By preparing a PowerPoint presentation for a district meeting, the following Common Core Anchor Standards for Speaking and Listening are also covered on page 122.

By recognizing how we can fit social justice–oriented social studies into language arts, teachers can outline for administration, parents, and colleagues how social justice goals for the classroom are aligned with the Common Core Standards in language arts. In this way, we are teaching an academically rigorous curriculum that meets grade-level standards and challenging our students to be critical and active thinkers.

Connecting to Common Core State Standards

Text Types and Purposes

- Write arguments to support claims in an analysis of substantive topics or texts, using valid reasoning and relevant and sufficient evidence.

Production and Distribution of Writing

- Produce clear and coherent writing in which the development, organization, and style are appropriate to task, purpose, and audience.
- Develop and strengthen writing as needed by planning, revising, editing, rewriting, or trying a new approach.
- Use technology, including the Internet, to produce and publish writing and to interact and collaborate with others.

Research to Build and Present Knowledge

- Gather relevant information from multiple print and digital sources, assess the credibility and accuracy of each source, and integrate the information while avoiding plagiarism.
- Draw evidence from literary or informational texts to support analysis, reflection, and research.

Connecting to Common Core State Standards

Presentation of Knowledge and Ideas

- Present information, findings, and supporting evidence such that listeners can follow the line of reasoning and the organization, development, and style are appropriate to task, purpose, and audience.
- Make strategic use of digital media and visual displays of data to express information and enhance understanding of presentations.

When facilitating action, we are working intentionally to promote social activism in the classroom by having students engage in a social action project that is particular to their school or community. By asking students to take action, we are reaffirming the role of youth in shaping the world today. We are providing a space for students to use their voices, their intellects, and their heart to change what they see as inequitable in this world. In this way students are engaged in a meaningful activity that is not only relevant to the standards that need to be covered but also applicable to students' day-to-day lives.

In the examples of teacher practice shared in this chapter, the teacher determines the strategy that students will use to make change, for example, letter writing. The teacher chooses the present-day social issue, guides students through the planning process, and engages students in social action. When planning your lesson on facilitating change, you can choose which pieces of the social action project you wish to control and which will emerge organically from students. Often, the more you allow your students to choose, the more meaningful and relevant the project will be to them. As a teacher, you must decide how much time you can allocate to this section of the framework and how you will structure the activity. Some questions you may ask yourself might include:

- How much time will I need for the activity?
- Will the project continue for many months or do I see this as only a 1- or 2-day lesson?
- If I am limited with time, could I have my students focus only on planning the project?
- What are my limitations with resources?

LETTER WRITING

Drawing on the previous lesson, past-to-present connections, we can ask students to examine which of the present-day issues seems most pertinent to their own day-to-day lives. For example, after learning about the American Civil War (1861–1865), also called the War Between the States, students may connect the Civil War to gang violence at their school. They may see the fight to end slavery as similar to their fight to end gang violence. Like those who resisted slavery in the past, this particular group of students hopes to resist gang violence by promoting safety and well-being at their school. For their social action project the class may decide to write a letter to their principal and district. Facilitated by their teacher, the class may engage in a series of minilessons to help them understand how to write a formal letter. The following questions could be taught as minilessons during a Writers' Workshop:

- How can we be persuasive and respectful in our writing?
- How do we structure a formal letter?
- How can we include quotes or anecdotes to make our letter personal?
- How can we include data in our letter to show evidence of how this social issue is affecting children and community members?

The class could interview students and include the students' quotes in the letter to make the letter personal. They could also accompany the letter with a signed petition. The letter-writing activity could meet the Common Core Anchor Standards for Writing on page 124.

Connect to Common Core State Standards

Production and Distribution of Writing

- Produce clear and coherent writing in which the development, organization, and style are appropriate to task, purpose, and audience.
- Develop and strengthen writing as needed by planning, revising, editing, rewriting, or trying a new approach.
- Use technology, including the Internet, to produce and publish writing and to interact and collaborate with others.

For many teachers, letter writing may be an appropriate strategy to meet standards and provide a space for students to take action. Students can write letters to community members about a concern they have for their neighborhood, to their principal about a school-based problem, and to congressional leaders about social issues such as the lack of access to adequate health care for their families. By providing a space for students to act, we are working to inspire in our students their capacity to be social change agents, while also being conscious of the standards we are expected to meet as teachers. In this next section, we see how John uses letter writing as a strategy to facilitate change in his classroom.

John's Classroom—The Rights of Migrants

We met John while learning strategies to help us paint the picture and connect the past to the present. John is a fifth-grade teacher in San Francisco. He used strategies such as artifact analysis, simulation, role play, graphic organizers, and read-alouds to help students see multiple perspectives surrounding the Great Depression. As a space for application, John had students pretend to be journalists writing newspaper articles. In the lesson in Chapter 5 John had students compare and contrast the Great Depression with our current recession by connecting the struggles of the past to the present in an open group discussion.

In this lesson, John builds on students' prior learning by asking them to recall what they had learned about the Great Depression from activities, slide shows, and their social studies book. John reads to students the story *Friends from the Other Side* (Anzaldúa, 1997), which tells the story of a friendship between a young Chicana, Prietita, and an undocumented immigrant boy, Joaquin. As John is reading students the story, he pauses often to ask them critical comprehension questions about the book such as: "Why did the boys pretend it was their choice to leave? Why do you think Joaquin has sores on his arms? Why did they hide from the police?"

John used the read-aloud as a platform to transition from conversations around the Great Depression and current recession to a social issue affecting many of his students' families today, the rights of migrant farmworkers. After finishing the book, John says to his students, "Today we are going to read real migrant workers' letters to the President."

John gives each pair of students two documents to read. The documents have students' names on them so that students will receive documents that are appropriate to their reading levels. After students have read their documents, they teach their partner about their primary source document, sharing what they have learned. Once students have completed this activity, John asks his students to write a letter to their congressional representative based on the documents they read and the discussions they had in class. In the persuasive letter, students ask their congressional representative to help migrant workers.

After students have completed their letters, John asks for volunteers to share their letter or something that interested them in their documents. He ends the lesson by asking students, "What did you learn about migrant farm workers?"

In this lesson, we can see how John provided structures for all students to access learning. He deliberately assigned document readings that were at each student's individual reading level and provided opportunities for students to share with partners, groups, and the whole class. He also tried to strategically pair students so that an English language learner was paired with a student who is proficient in their primary language and English.

John created a strong link between language arts and social studies. John leans on a read-aloud to provide students with background information around the treatment of migrant farmworkers. He has students write letters to their congressional representative, allowing students to express social justice ideals and learn an important tool, writing formal letters.

The focus of this lesson was for students to understand who migrant farm-workers are, what they do, and how they are treated. John draws on primary documents as a means for students to understand the everyday lived experiences of those who work in the field. Since John's students and their parents or family members may be or know migrant farmworkers, it might be helpful to engage students by asking, "What do you know about migrant farmworkers? Do you think they are treated fairly? Why or why not? What could you do to fight for the rights of migrant farmworkers? How have farmworkers resisted unfair treatment in the past?" In this way we are working directly to connect content to the day-to-day lives of our students. We are also posing a question in such a way that students can feel responsible and empowered to fight for the rights of others.

For John to meet the language arts Common Core Standards and facilitate change, John needs to explicitly teach students how to write a formal letter. To teach letter writing, John needs to model letter writing for students, share some examples of formal letters, provide sentence frames (which is particularly helpful to English language learners), and allow his students time for editing, revising, and typing a formal letter. If John engaged students in minilessons around letter writing specifically aligned with the language arts Common Core Standards for fifth grade and gave students the opportunity to revise and edit their letters through the Writers' Workshop process (covered in Chapter 4), John could meet the following ELA Common Core Standards for Writing, grade 5:

Connecting to Common Core State Standards

Text Types and Purposes for W.5.1

W.5.1. Write opinion pieces on topics or texts, supporting a point of view with reasons and information.
  - Introduce a topic or text clearly, state an opinion, and create an organizational structure in which ideas are logically grouped to support the writer's purpose.
  - Provide logically ordered reasons that are supported by facts and details.
  - Link opinion and reasons using words, phrases, and clauses (e.g., *consequently, specifically*).
  - Provide a concluding statement or section related to the opinion presented.

Production and Distribution of Writing

W.5.4. Produce clear and coherent writing in which the development and organization are appropriate to task, purpose, and audience.
W.5.5. With guidance and support from peers and adults, develop and strengthen writing as needed by planning, revising, editing, rewriting, or trying a new approach.
W.5.6. With some guidance and support from adults, use technology, including the Internet, to produce and publish writing as well as to interact and collaborate with others; demonstrate sufficient command of keyboarding skills to type a minimum of two pages in a single sitting.

In this case, John could meet the language arts Common Core Standards and facilitate change in the classroom by explicitly teaching letter writing and providing a space for students to resist the unfair working conditions for migrant workers.

Jen's Classroom—Distribution of Corporate Progits and Wealth

We met Jen in Chapter 5. She is a fourth-grade teacher in San Francisco, who designed a curriculum unit that studies the building of the Transcontinental Railroad from the Chinese perspective. In connecting the past to the present, Jen highlighted past issues of injustice to current issues of exploitation through a slide show and discussion around the treatment of people in sweatshops and unfair wages. In this lesson Jen asks students to draw on their prior learning to write a letter to the Nike CEO, telling him what they think and feel about the treatment of Nike workers.

Jen begins the lesson by passing out a blank sheet of paper and crayons to each student, except for two. The papers are numbered, with either a 1, 2, or 3. She asks students who have paper and crayons to begin drawing flowers. She then explains that the two students without paper are going to be supervisors. The role of the supervisors is to walk around the classroom and make sure the class is working hard to draw beautiful flowers.

After a few minutes Jen asks students to bring their drawings of flowers to the front of the room. Papers with a number 1 are awarded 20 pretzels, papers with a number 2 are awarded 8 pretzels, and papers with a number 3 are given a crumb. After each student has been given his or her share of the pretzels, the supervisors are awarded with large overflowing bags of pretzels as an award for their job well done. Jen asks students to think about the following question: "You all painted beautiful flowers and were not paid the same amount for your work. Why is this unfair?"

Jen used this activity as a means for students to think back to the previous day's lesson about the unfair treatment of labor workers in sweatshops. She says to the class, "When we come across unjust things in life, we can and should speak up and act out against them." She explains to students that they are going to take a closer look at one of the companies they talked about yesterday: Nike. She shows students clips from the video *Behind the Swoosh: Sweatshops and Social Justice* (Keady & Kretzu, 2004). The video details Nike's environmental and labor practices and how people against Nike's practices speak up and take action against what is unfair and unjust.

After the video Jen gathers her students on the floor for a discussion about the film. She asks them, "Why do you think Nike may not want to disclose how much they pay their employees? Do you think this is right? What could happen if they do disclose this information? Is this information important? Could we do more to help the Nike workers if we had this information?"

Following the discussion, Jen asks her students to write a rough draft of a letter to Nike about what they think and how they feel about the company and its actions. She reminds students to refer back to the word walls and graphic organizers created in class to remember important words and key concepts such as *exploitation* or *wage*. She gives students 10–15 minutes to write their draft and then asks them to underline a word or phrase in their letter that they wish to share with the class. Students then sit in a circle and share their word or phrase with the class one at a time.

Jen closes the lesson by saying:

> You all have strong feelings and opinions about Nike. Thank you for sharing. We should make our voices heard and share this information with others. As a class we are going to create a newsletter to share with the whole school and parents about what we know about Nike, how we feel about this information, and what we are going to do now because of it. In this newsletter we need to make sure to put facts and information that we learned about Nike and its workers. We also need to make sure that we put what each of us thinks or feels about this.

For homework Jen asks students to think about what they might want the newsletter to look like and what they think is important to put in it.

In this lesson we can see how Jen makes a strong transition between connecting the past and the present and facilitating change. She draws from previous conversations around exploitations, sweatshops, and unfair wages to concentrate on one specific corporation and their treatment of workers. She integrates literacy by having students write letters to the CEO of Nike and then extending the letter writing into a newsletter addressed to the school and community.

Jen also uses a simulation activity as a reminder to students of what it means to be treated unfairly. She carries the idea of injustice throughout all five lessons in the framework, building from the unfair treatment of Chinese workers building the Transcontinental Railroad to a present-day examination of the unfair treatment of workers in sweatshops. Jen also uses a video as a tool to build students' background knowledge around the environmental and labor practices of Nike. The video also helped to review concepts studied during the unit, such as "wage" and "discrimination," by providing visual representations, which could be especially helpful for English language learners in the classroom.

Like John, Jen could have made more explicit the ties between all five lessons in her closure. She could remind students that discriminatory practices existed in the past and they still exist today. She could also remind students that ordinary people like us resisted inequality in the past to make a better life for us today. We too can fight injustices so that we can make a better future for others.

Also, like John, if Jen could allot more time to the letter-writing activity and teach minilessons that are aligned with the language arts Common Core Standards, such as teaching students to support their arguments or supporting reasons with facts and details, Jen may be able to facilitate change and meet mandated standards. For example, if Jen allowed students to work through the writing process of prewriting, drafting, revising, editing, and publishing (detailed in Chapter 4) and supported their learning with minilessons on formal letter writing, Jen could meet the following ELA Common Core Standards for Writing, grade 4:

Connecting to Common Core State Standards

Text Types and Purposes

W.4.1. Write opinion pieces on topics or texts, supporting a point of view with reasons and information.

- Introduce a topic or text clearly, state an opinion, and create an organizational structure in which related ideas are grouped to support the writer's purpose.
- Provide reasons that are supported by facts and details.
- Link opinion and reasons using words and phrases (e.g., *for instance, in order to, in addition*).
- Provide a concluding statement or section related to the opinion presented.

Production and Distribution of Writing

W.4.4. Produce clear and coherent writing in which the development and organization are appropriate to task, purpose, and audience.

W.4.5. With guidance and support from peers and adults, develop and strengthen writing as needed by planning, revising, and editing.

W.4.6. With some guidance and support from adults, use technology, including the Internet, to produce and publish writing as well as to interact and collaborate with others; demonstrate sufficient command of keyboarding skills to type a minimum of one page in a single sitting.

As teachers may be limited with time, suggesting a final project such as letter writing may be the easiest way to both facilitate change and meet time requirements. It is often beneficial to allow students the opportunity to choose which person they want to write to and what they plan to say in the letter. By explicitly teaching standards and providing a space for students to resist what is unfair and unjust, a teacher could integrate language arts and social studies content, meet language arts Common Core Standards, and provide a space for students to make change in their schools and communities.

For our younger learners, we could use the strategy of letter writing as a shared writing activity. The teacher does the writing on a piece of chart paper while students share with their teacher what they want to write. Teacher and students go through the writing process collaboratively, revising drafts based on feedback. Teachers could also provide sentence frames as a means of supporting English language learners in the classroom.

Once students are finished with their letters, prepare the letters to be sent out. Remind students that there is great power in numbers, and that we should encourage our friends and family to write letters as well. Students may also submit a petition with their letter, showing how many people are against the action being made in schools and communities.

Letters could also be just the beginning of a social action project. For example, maybe students wanted a garden at their school where they could grow fresh fruits and vegetables to be used to prepare their school lunches. The students could collaboratively devise an action plan, draft letters to community businesses to solicit materials, follow up with letters and phone calls, and have face-to-face meetings. In looking at the language arts Common Core Standards, each of these components of social change could be connected to standards listed under Listening and Speaking, Writing, and Reading. Facilitating change in the classroom does not have to feel disconnected from the expectations we have as teachers, but rather as integrated and deeply connected to our day-to-day work.

PERFORMANCE AND ART

Art and performance can be important aspects of facilitating change in the classroom. For English language learners, art and performance can provide a medium for students to express themselves when English written language may feel limiting. This section highlights the lessons of two teachers, each who used performance and art to facilitate discussions surrounding change in the classroom.

Kendra's Classroom—Conservation and the Community

Kendra is a third-grade teacher in San Francisco, California. For social studies, Kendra is expected to teach students about local geography, including a study of communities. Prior to this lesson, students engaged in an exploration of communities through picture and text, a group activity that required students to develop their own community. Students also learned about maps through exploration and geography. In this lesson Kendra brings a close to the unit through a lesson that works to facilitate change by asking students to consider ways they can conserve the environment.

The lesson begins with Kendra asking her students, "Let's reflect on the last lesson: How do human-use and man-made structures affect the environment?" After Kendra lists her students' answers on the board, she transitions to a read-aloud, *Common Ground: The Water, Earth, and Air We Share* (Bang, 1997).

While she is reading the book, she pauses to ask students questions about how we might be contributing to the depletion of natural resources. Once the read-aloud is finished, Kendra introduces the word *pollution* and puts the word up on the word wall. She asks students if they can give examples of pollution.

She notes to students that they will define *pollution* as anything that makes a natural resource dirty or unsafe to use. She puts up pictures of water, air, and trash pollution on the overhead as examples of different types of pollution. Next, she states her objective, "Today we will be discussing the different ways that people add to the problem of pollution."

Kendra then puts up a picture of a landfill and asks students to look at some of the things present in the landfills. Kendra adds the word *landfill* to the wall. She asks students to share what types of things can be recycled so that they can minimize the amount of waste that goes into landfills. Together, Kendra and her class look at the pictures of landfills to investigate what could have been recycled.

Kendra continues to highlight different environmental issues that might be affecting the community, including logging and decreased water levels. Next, Kendra shifts to a discussion around *conservation*, also adding this word to the word wall. Together as a class, Kendra and her students discuss what *conservation* means and how they can do their part to help conserve the environment.

Kendra then plays the video *Change the World in 5 Minutes—Every Day at School* (Bancks, 2009) to learn about some things that can be done by everyone, including kids, to live green and conserve. After watching the video, students brainstorm ideas of how they can conserve.

Kendra asks students to get into groups of four and choose one method of conservation to role play for the class. Each group shares their skit. After the role play activity is finished, students reflect on what they learned about conservation as a class and what they can do to recycle or practice conservation at school and/or in their homes. Kendra ends the lesson by asking students to write a letter to a friend, parent, or relative informing them about issues in the environment and ways that they can help by recycling or conserving water. Kendra tells students that she will mail each of the letters. Once the letters are written, Kendra asks students to share a few sentences about what they wrote in their letters.

In this lesson Kendra draws from what students know about their community and the natural resources that surround them to have a discussion on what students can do to protect their environment. Kendra deepens the discussion by asking students to role-play ways in which they may practice conservation and also has students write letters to friends and family members informing them of how they can participate in protecting our environment.

We can also see how Kendra provided intentional structured support for her English language learners. She frontloaded vocabulary and provided a word wall with visual representations that students could access throughout the lesson. Kendra also used other visual representations throughout her lesson including a read-aloud, video, and various photos and images to support the content.

Kendra could extend this lesson with a discussion around environmental injustice. *Environmental injustice* is a term used to describe the disproportionately higher number of people of color subjected to environmental health risks compared to other groups in society. In communities where people of color live, there is an increased chance of toxic landfills, incinerators, industrial dumping, and other environmental hazards (Kozol, 1995).

Students could look analytically at the placement of landfills and research where landfills are located and why. Students could also study where large factories are built and their proximity to schools in low-income areas. Wade (2007) affirms, "Our students can learn from many examples of environmental injustices as well as from stories of action taken by citizens and governments to preserve our natural resources" (p. 57). By teaching students about environmental injustice in connection with lessons about communities, Kendra could cover her social studies standards, which expect her to teach about communities and the environment, and provide students opportunities to critically examine how environmental laws may be working to serve some and hurt others.

To meet the Common Core language arts standards for third grade and still teach social justice–oriented social studies content, Kendra could explicitly teach her students how to write an informative/explanatory letter to their friends and family. Through minilessons, Kendra could detail for her students how to introduce a topic, integrate illustrations, develop the topic with details, and provide a concluding statement. After each minilesson, students have the opportunity to translate what they learned into their writing. Each informative/explanatory text goes through the writing process. If Kendra presented the writing assignment to her students in this way, she could meet the following ELA Common Core Standards for Writing, grade 3:

Connecting to Common Core State Standards

Text Types and Purposes

W.3.2. Write informative/explanatory texts to examine a topic and convey ideas and information clearly.
  - Introduce a topic and group related information together; include illustrations when useful to aiding comprehension.
  - Develop the topic with facts, definitions, and details.
  - Use linking words and phrases (e.g., *also, another, and, more, but*) to connect ideas within categories of information.
  - Provide a concluding statement or section.

By being conscious of the language arts standards, Kendra could potentially address and integrate social studies content into language arts. In this way Kendra might have a better chance of finding time and opportunities to teach social justice–oriented social studies curriculum.

Susan's Classroom—Positive Graffiti

We met Susan, a fourth-grade teacher in San Francisco, while painting the picture in Chapter 3. She used a simulation as an initial introduction to the treatment of the Chinese at Angel Island as a result of the Chinese Exclusion Act in 1882 and then painted the picture for her students through the use of read-alouds and a field trip to Angel Island. In this lesson Susan facilitates change by having students draft a "graffiti poem," a piece of artwork portraying their hope for change.

Susan begins the lesson by asking her students to consider the following questions in their table groups:

- What is graffiti?
- What is the difference between graffiti and art?
- Do you think what the detainees wrote on the walls at Angel Island was graffiti or art?

Once students finish their discussions, Susan projects a copy of one of the poems from Angel Island. Susan reads the poem to her class, pausing to unpack vocabulary words. After reading the poem, Susan projects a picture by Banksy, a famous England-based graffiti artist, and asks her students, "What do you see? What is this picture saying?"

Susan explains to her students that there are many reasons that people are drawn toward public artistic expression, whether it is an image or in written form (or both). She asks her students, "Why might someone want to express themselves artistically?" and writes her students' answers on the board. Susan then returns to some of the themes that continually emerged from the poems written on walls of the detention center at Angel Island:

- Daily life in detention
- Homesickness, family values, guilt, obligations
- Regret for coming to America
- Resentment over treatment
- Encouragement, support for fellow detainees, consolation
- Warning, advice
- Promoting the common good: peace, love, equality
- Speaking out about injustice: bringing awareness, educating

- Standing up for the oppressed
- Inspiring others: beauty
- Sharing experiences, values, hopes
- Showing solidarity

Susan explains that everyone has something special to say, something important to tell others, a point of view that matters. She asks her students to choose one of the themes from the Angel Island poems and brainstorm, using a web, ideas connected to the theme. She explains to students that each of the themes were issues that the Chinese in detainment had to deal with. Although the list is particular to the poems the Chinese wrote at Angel Island, many of these issues are connected to present-day social issues as well.

Susan models the activity for her students. She takes the theme "Standing up for the oppressed" and writes it in the middle of the page in a circle, drawing lines out from it labeled *marches, the poor, war, read,* and so on. The teacher emphasizes that the goal is to write (or draw) the first things that come to mind.

After students make webs of the theme they chose, students then continue to work individually and in pairs to develop their idea into a poem and/or an image, which will be called "graffiti." Students are expected to integrate their point of view into the artwork and express their beliefs behind the social issue they chose. After students finish their "graffiti" piece, they share their art with the class. Their artwork is then displayed in the classroom for others to see.

In this lesson Susan facilitates change in her classroom by providing an activity for her students that allows them to articulate into art their emotions around injustice. Susan carefully bridges prior learning to new content by drawing intentionally on the poems students read on the walls of Angel Island in the lesson before. She reminds students of the poems and delineates themes that were depicted throughout the poems. Susan then asks students to brainstorm and think about how this theme is relevant to their lives today. Art, in this way, is not only a medium of expression, but also a powerful tool for students to use to share their ideas and thoughts.

Some may consider Susan's activity to be a "fun activity"; however, if we review the Common Core Standards for fourth grade, Susan is meeting many of the standards for Speaking and Listening. For example, Susan provides multiple opportunities for students to engage in a wide variety of collaborative discussions, allowing students to develop and share their ideas with one another. The lesson also builds on students' prior learning, asking them to remember and recognize what they had learned about Angel Island to help them brainstorm and build their graffiti poems. Through her lesson, Susan could cover the following ELA Common Core Standards for Speaking and Listening, grade 4, on the next page.

In addition to the two strategies to facilitate change discussed in this section, role play and graffiti art, students could also create signs to hang around

Connecting to Common Core State Standards
Comprehension and Collaboration
SL.4.1. Engage effectively in a range of collaborative discussions (one-on-one, in groups, and teacher-led) with diverse partners on *grade 4 topics and texts*, building on others' ideas and expressing their own clearly.
Pose and respond to specific questions to clarify or follow up on information, and make comments that contribute to the discussion and link to the remarks of others.
Review the key ideas expressed and explain their own ideas and understanding in light of the discussion.

the school portraying their point of view. For example, a class that wished for more physical exercise during the school day might make signs showing the consequences of obesity and the benefits of promoting health and fitness at school.

CONCLUSION

In social justice–oriented social studies lessons, we challenge students to examine historical content from multiple perspectives and determine for themselves what happened in history. We also challenge students to think analytically about what it means to live in a socially just world. And we provide students with opportunities to question the status quo, hoping to arouse in them a desire to make change in their schools and communities. Through social justice–oriented social studies lessons, students begin to see and name injustices that exist within the world around them and spaces where they can take significant steps to make change. An important piece of teaching for social justice is for students to not only see, but to work to alter and transform the world through social action projects. Social action is particularly meaningful to students when relevant to students' daily lives and linked to the content learned in school. In this chapter, we discussed ways to facilitate change in your classroom. We also discussed ways in which to teach social justice–oriented social studies content and meet language arts Common Core Standards.

Facilitating change, the last tenet of the framework, is designed to help teachers think about ways in which students can make an explicit connection between what they are studying in class and real-world issues. Students draw from the past-to-present connections they determined in previous lessons to focus on a particular social issue that is affecting them directly. Facilitated by the teacher, students work collaboratively in groups or as a class to plan and implement a social action project designed to resist injustice. As discussed earlier, some teachers may determine a specific social action project for students to pursue, while others may wish for the social action project to emerge organically from the students. In each way, teachers facilitate a space for students to make change. Social action projects might include the following: students writing letters to their city council member asking them to shut down the liquor store across the street from their school; students planning a sit-in designed to peacefully protest the unhealthy lunches provided at their school; or students making signs to defend or attack policy they perceive as just or unjust. By facilitating change in the classroom, teachers give students the opportunity to collaborate, organize, and take action.

As teachers, we facilitate change in the classroom by asking students to find injustices they want to change. However, to be able to find and name injustices, students must have opportunities to question the status quo and roots of injustice. If students have opportunities to critically analyze injustice, but then do not have the opportunity to act, students may leave our classrooms feeling depleted and helpless. Bigelow, Harvey, and Karp (2004) affirm this, saying, "If we ask children to critique the world but then fail to encourage them to act, our classrooms can degenerate into factories of cynicism" (p. 4). Students may feel powerless in their capability to make change. For this reason, we must connect stories of struggle to stories of resistance. We must also continually remind our students that they too can alter and change the world just as their ancestors did. We want our students to see themselves as change makers and to act to make a difference. Our students can draw inspiration from the historical and contemporary efforts of those who struggled for justice, including the models of resistance presented during lessons that served to inspire wonder and paint the picture.

Included in this chapter are questions that can help students organize their social action projects. The questions ask students to consider resources they need, obstacles they may confront, and organizations and people they can lean on. Students can also draw on their own experience as they plan their steps toward action, making learning directly linked to students' experiences an integral part of the curriculum.

In terms of connecting language arts and social studies, we found multiple ways to meet language arts Common Core Standards and connect social studies content through a social action project. As most of these projects require reading and writing (e.g., creating a newspaper, writing a letter, preparing a speech), look at the Common Core Standards for language arts or your state standards to see which ones are being covered. Finished products such as letters, articles, or printed speeches can serve as valuable tools for assessment. As we continue to teach language arts and social studies as complementary subjects, we offer students the opportunity to engage in meaningful learning that supports students in becoming critical, active thinkers as well as strong, technical readers.

When facilitating change in the classroom and empowering students to engage in social action projects, it is important to remind our students that fighting for social change is difficult, complex, and often daunting work. As Perry and Fraser (1993) note, "we hold on to the dream while simultaneously acknowledging the limits of the world we must struggle in" (p. 208). Facilitating change in the classroom is centered on possibility. In our classrooms, we work collaboratively to model for ourselves and others what it is like when we all join in an effort to help one another. We engage in social action because we feel a responsibility toward ourselves and others, including a belief that we can pass on a better world to future generations. We take hope in the fact that things can be different and we can play a role, even if a small one, in making change. We remind each other that each of us has the vision, skills, commitment, courage, and perseverance to work toward a better world. By facilitating change in the classroom, we empower our students to collaborate, organize, and take action, reaffirming the role of students in shaping the world today, and thus we provide our students a greater promise, hope, and possibility for the future.

REFLECTION EXERCISES

Below are reflection exercises to help extend these concepts into classroom practice:

1. How might you transition from connecting the past to the present to discussions around facilitating change? Why is it important to facilitate change? Why is it important for your students to see themselves as change agents?
2. How might a social action project meet some of the language arts Common Core Standards? Which standards could you meet?
3. How will you carve out space for a social action project?
4. How will you support students through their social action project? What resources will you make available?
5. What can students learn from studying other people's struggles and acts of resistance in the past? How might this help them organize and plan their steps toward action?

Conclusion

S OCIAL JUSTICE-ORIENTED SOCIAL studies classrooms, in their greatest capacity, are laboratories of democracy, educating students to employ skills such as critical thinking, collaboration, problem solving, decision making, and data analysis as key inquiry processes that will help them work to sustain and improve a democratic way of life (National Council for the Social Studies, 2012).

In a social justice–oriented social studies classroom, students learn to analyze, question, and determine for themselves what really happened in history. History is portrayed as a wealth of complex and controversial issues, "where there is no right and wrong, no experts, and one's opinion may be as good as another's" (Au et al., 2007, p. 181). Teachers challenge students to critically think about texts they read by raising questions such as: Who or what is absent from this text? Who stands to benefit or be hurt from this text? How is language used in specific ways to convey specific ideas in this text?

We take intentional steps to bring to the surface the voices of those who have been historically silenced and marginalized in our textbooks. By teaching multiple perspectives, teachers encourage students to see that there are multiple stories that can be told about any event (Wade, 2007). As students see and hear the contributions and actions of their ancestors, students may be more empowered and motivated to make change in their own communities. Students may also feel empowered by others' stories of struggle and resistance to serve as allies and help others in their fight for justice. As we integrate the histories of all people into the curriculum, we simultaneously teach our students to analyze, read, learn, and ask questions about the world. Our classrooms embrace pluralism as we create and enact curriculum inclusive of the needs of our diverse students. As teachers, we draw from the contributions and lived experiences of all our learners and build solidarity in the classroom by drawing threads between our similarities and differences, past and present.

To teach social studies for social justice may require "creative adaption, thoughtful resistance, and compromise" (Wade, 2007, p. 35). For some, this may require introducing fewer social studies events/topics and examining them more critically and/or finding ways to integrate social studies content into language arts. Teachers will need to be conscious of both social studies district and state standards and the language arts Common Core Standards so they can find ways to merge their commitment to social justice–oriented teaching with the expectations of administration. As teachers, our conscious-ness around standards will help us enrich our teaching and maintain strong academic teaching and learning for all of our students. By reconceptualizing the way we teach social studies, we may be better able to navigate standards and test-driven environments to develop social justice curriculum

Finding allies within your school and community with whom you can share ideas, resources, and challenges may provide great support for you as you move forward with your vision of social justice. Grassroots organizations such as Teachers 4 Social Justice (San Francisco), New York Collective of Radical Educators (New York), or Teachers for Social Justice (Chicago) and other organizations such as the National Association for Multicultural Edu-cation (NAME) advocate for equity and social justice through multicultural education. Memberships in these organizations may provide you with the support you need to move forward with your visions of teaching, a space to push against district and state policy that may not promote equity within your school, a chance to meet like-minded folks, and the opportunity to gain and share lesson plan ideas and resources.

As we teach for social justice, we work toward a better and different fu-ture. Our work as educators, combined with our effort to teach for equity and change, is an essential step toward fighting injustice. We can remain resilient in our efforts to teach for social justice by finding hope in the possibility and potential for social change. We can find hope as we see our students learn to question the status quo and work to make change within their schools and communities. We can find hope as we learn to work together as teachers to creatively integrate social justice ideals into the curriculum and navigate con-straints such as standardization and accountability. And we can find hope as we work in solidarity with our community members to take action toward un-just policies and change what is unfair. It is through our resilience, hope, and actions that we will make positive change in this world and promise a better future for our children.

References

Adams, M., Bell, L., & Griffin, P. (Eds.). (1997). *Teaching for diversity and social justice*. New York: Routledge.

Agarwal, R. (2012). Perceiving possibility in teaching for social justice: Finding hope without illusion. *Journal of Multiculturalism in Education, 7*(3).

Agarwal, R., Epstein, S., Oppenheim, R., Oyler, C., & Sonu, D. (2010). From ideal to practice and back again: Beginning teachers teaching for social justice. *Journal of Teacher Education, 61*(3), 237–247.

Anzaldúa, G. (1997). *Friends from the other side*. New York: Children's Book Press.

Asher, J. (1969). The total physical response approach to second language learning. *The Modern Language Journal, 53*(1), 3–17.

Au, W. (2009). The "building tasks" of critical history: Structuring social studies for social justice, *Social Studies Research and Practice, (4)*2, 25–35.

Au, W., Bigelow, B., & Karp, S. (Eds.). (2007). *Rethinking our classrooms: Teaching for equity and justice* (Vol. 1). Milwaukee, WI: Rethinking Schools.

Ayers, W. (2001) *To teach: The journey of a teacher*. New York: Teachers College Press.

Bancks, T. (2009). *Change the world in 5 minutes—every day at school* [Video]. Retrieved from http://www.tristanbancks.com/p/video.html

Bang, M. (1997). *Common ground: The water, earth, and air we share*. New York: Blue Sky Press.

Bigelow, B., Harvey, B., & Karp, S. (Eds.). (2004). *Rethinking our classrooms: Teaching for equity and justice* (Vol. 2). Milwaukee, WI: Rethinking Schools.

Bigelow, B., & Peterson, B. (Eds.). (1998). *Rethinking Columbus: The next 500 years* (2nd ed.). Milwaukee, WI: Rethinking Schools.

Bridges, R. (1999). *Through my eyes*. New York: Scholastic Press.

Burant, T., Christensen, L. Salas, K., & Walters, S. (Eds.). (2010). *The new teacher book: Finding purpose, balance, and hope during your first years in the classroom* (2nd ed.). Milwaukee, WI: Rethinking Schools.

Calkins, L. (1994). *The art of teaching writing*. Portsmouth, NH: Heinemann.

Castillo, E. (2011). Short overview of California Indian history. *California Native American Heritage Commission*. Retrieved from http://www.nahc.ca.gov/califindian.html

Chen, L., & Mora-Flores, E. (2006). *Balanced literacy for English language learners, K–2*. Portsmouth, NH: Heinemann.

Christensen, L. (2009). *Teaching for joy and justice: Re-imagining the language arts classroom*. Milwaukee, WI: Rethinking Schools.

Coerr, E. (1977). *Sadako and the thousand paper cranes*. New York: Putnam.

Common Core State Standards Initiative. (2012). Retrieved from http://www.corestandards.org/ELA-Literacy

Cornelissen, C. (1998). *Soft rain: A story of the Cherokee trail of tears*. New York: Bantam Doubleday Dell Books for Young Readers.

Cowhey, M. (2006). *Black ants and Buddhists: Teaching critically and teaching differently in the primary grades*. Portland, ME: Stenhouse Publishers.

Cuthrell, K., & Yates, P. (2007). Making it all fit: Integration strategies for social studies and literacy. *Delta Kappa Gamma Bulletin, 73*(4), 22–39.

Darling-Hammond, L., French, J., & Garcia-Lopez, S. (Eds.). (2002). *Learning to teach for social justice.* New York: Teachers College Press.

Echevarria, J., & Graves, A. (2007). *Sheltered content instruction: Teaching English language learners with diverse abilities.* Boston: Pearson Education.

Echevarria, J., Vogt, M., & Short, D. (2004). *Making content comprehensible for English learners: The SIOP model.* Boston: Pearson Education.

Gonzalez, M., Moll, L., & Amanti, C. (2005). *Funds of knowledge: Theorizing practices in households, communities, and classrooms.* Mahwah, NJ: Erlbaum.

Gordon, L. (2009). *Dorothea Lange: A life beyond limits.* New York: Norton.

Hursh, D., & Ross, E. (Eds.). (2000). *Democratic social education: Social studies for social change.* New York: Falmer Press.

Johnson, E. (2007). Critical literacy and the social studies methods course: How preservice teachers learn and teach for critical literacy. *Social Studies Research and Practice, 2*(2), 145–168.

Johnson, G. (2008, November 17). Critics' picks: The grapes of wrath [Video]. *The New York Times.* Retrieved from http://www.nytimes.com/video/2008/11/17/movies/1194832268537/critics-picks-the-grapes-of-wrath.html

Keady, J., & Kretzu, L. (2004). *Behind the swoosh: Sweatshops and social justice* [Video]. United States: Educating for Justice.

Keene, E., & Zimmerman, S. (2007). *Mosaic of thought: The power of comprehension strategy* (2nd ed.). Portsmouth, NH: Heinemann.

Kent, A., & Simpson, J. (2008). Social studies and literacy integration: making the most of our teaching. *Social Studies Research and Practice, 3*(1), 142–152. Retrieved from http://www.socstrp.org/issues/PDF/3.1.12.pdf

Kornfeld, J., & Leyden, G. (2005). Acting out: Literature, drama, and connecting with history. *International Reading Association, 59*(3), 230–238.

Kozol, J. (1995). *Amazing grace: The lives of children and the conscience of the nation.* New York: Harper Perennial.

Krull, K. (2003). *Harvesting hope: The story of Cesar Chavez.* Boston: Harcourt Children's Books.

Ladson-Billings, G. (1994). *Dreamkeepers: Successful teachers of African-American children.* San Francisco: Jossey-Bass.

Lai, M., Lim, G., & Yung, J. (1991). *Island Poetry and History of Chinese Immigrants on Angel Island, 1910-1940.* Seattle: University of Washington Press.

Lalas, J. (2007). Teaching for social justice in multicultural urban schools: Conceptualization and classroom implication. *Multicultural Education, 14*(3), 17–21.

Lee, E., Menkart, D., & Okazawa-Rey, M. (Eds.). (2007). *Beyond heroes and holidays: A practical guide to K–12 anti-racist, multicultural education and staff development* (2nd ed.). Washington, DC: Teaching for Change.

Lee, M., & Choi, Y. (2006). *Landed.* Vancouver, BC, Canada: Douglas & McIntyre.

Levstik, L., & Barton, K. (2005). *Doing history: Investigating with children in elementary and middle schools.* Mahwah, NJ: Erlbaum.

Loewen, J. (2007). *Lies my teacher told me. Everything your American history textbooks got wrong.* New York: Simon & Schuster.

Loewen, J. (2010). *Teaching what really happened: How to avoid the tyranny of textbooks and get students excited about doing history.* New York: Teachers College Press.

McKissack, P. (2011) *Dear America: A picture of freedom.* New York: Scholastic Press.

Menkart, D., Murray, A., & View, J. (2004). *Putting the movement back into civil rights teaching.* Washington, DC: Teaching for Change.

National Council for the Social Studies. (2012). *National curriculum standards for social studies: Introduction.* Retrieved from http://www.socialstudies.org/standards/introduction

Oakes, J., & Lipton, M. (2007). *Teaching to change the world* (3rd ed.). Boston: McGraw Hill.

Ogle, D. M. (1986). K-W-L: A teaching model that develops active reading of expository text. *Reading Teacher, 39,* 564–570.

Ozick, C. (1989). *Metaphor and memory.* New York: Knopf Doubleday.

Perry, T., & Fraser, J. (Eds.). (1993). *Teaching in the multicultural classroom: Freedom's plow.* London: Routledge.

Ray, K., & Cleaveland, L. (2004). *About the authors: Writing workshop with our youngest writers.* Portsmouth, NH: Heinemann.

Robinson, A. (1997). *A street called home.* Chicago: Harcourt Brace.

Scharer, P., & Pinnell, G. (2008). *Guiding K–3 writers to independence: The new essentials.* New York: Scholastic.

Schmidt, P. (1999). KWLQ: Inquiry and literacy learning in science. *The Reading Teacher, 52*(7), 789-792.

Schmidt, L. (2007). *Social studies that sticks: How to bring content and concepts to life.* Portsmouth, NH: Heinemann.

Seidman, L. (1976). *The fools of '49: The California Gold Rush, 1848–1856.* New York: Random House Childrens Books.

Shor, I. (1992). *Empowering education: Critical teaching for social change.* Chicago: University of Chicago Press.

Singer, D., & Singer, J. (1992). *The house of make-believe: Children's play and the developing imagination.* Boston: Harvard University Press.

Sleeter, C. (2005). *Un-standardizing curriculum: Multicultural teaching in the standards-based classroom.* New York: Teachers College Press.

Sleeter, C. (2011). *The academic and social value of ethnic studies: A review of research.* Washington, DC: National Education Association.

Sunal, C., & Haas, M. (2008). *Social studies for the elementary and middle grades: A constructivist approach.* (3rd ed.) Boston: Pearson Education.

Takaki, R. (2008). *A different mirror: A history of multicultural America.* Boston: Back Bay Books.

Tompkins, G. (2010). *Literacy for the 21st century: A balanced approach.* Boston: Allyn & Bacon.

Uschan, M. (2002). *The California Gold Rush.* New York: Gareth Stevens.

VanSledright, B. (2002). *In search of America's past: Learning to read history in elementary school.* New York: Teachers College Press.

Wade, R. (2007). *Social studies for social justice: Teaching strategies for the elementary classroom.* New York: Teachers College Press.

Williams, J. (2005). *The Miwok of California.* New York: Powerkids Press.

Wolk, S. (2003). Teaching for critical literacy in social studies. *The Social Studies, 94*(3), 101–106.

Wormser, R. (2002). *Jim Crow stories: The Great Depression* (1929–1939). The rise and fall of Jim Crow. Retrieved from http://www.pbs.org/wnet/jimcrow/stories_events_depression.html

Yee, P., & Ng, S. (2011). *Tales from gold mountain.* Toronto: Groundwood Books. (Original work published 1989)

Yin. (2003). *Coolies.* New York: Puffin.

Yolen, J. (1996). *Encounter.* San Anselmo: Sandpiper Press.

Zinn, H. (2003). *A people's history of the United States.* New York: HarperCollins.

Index

About the Author

Ruchi Agarwal-Rangnath procured her doctorate in education from Teachers College, Columbia University. She currently is an adjunct professor in Elementary Education at San Francisco State University, where she teaches courses in literacy, social studies, and multicultural education. Agarwal-Rangnath presently is vice president of the National Association of Multicultural Education, California Chapter (NAME-CA). She has worked as a teacher educator and elementary school teacher in various urban schools in California and New York. She also works as a consultant, providing professional development to schools working to develop and enrich their mission of teaching toward equity and social justice.